C000082187

Think It Not Strange: Navigating Trials in the New America

Copyright © 2016 by Desiring God

Download this book in three digital formats,
free of charge, at desiringGod.org

Published by Desiring God
Post Office Box 2901
Minneapolis, MN 55402

Unless otherwise indicated, Scripture quotations are from the
ESV Bible (*The Holy Bible, English Standard Version*), copyright
2001 by Crossway. Used by permission. All rights reserved.

All emphases in Scripture quotations have
been added by the author or editor.

ISBN: 978-0-9912776-9-8
Cover design: Taylor Design Works
eBook design: Josh Pritchard, Gideon House Books
Typesetting: Ryan Leichty
First printing 2016
Printed in the United States of America

Beloved, do not be surprised at the fiery trial when it comes upon you to test you, as though something strange were happening to you. But rejoice insofar as you share Christ's sufferings, that you may also rejoice and be glad when his glory is revealed. If you are insulted for the name of Christ, you are blessed, because the Spirit of glory and of God rests upon you.
—1 Peter 4:12–14

CONTENTS

CONTRIBUTORS

BOB BLINCOE is the president of Frontiers USA in Phoenix, Arizona. He previously was US Director of Frontiers for fifteen years. In 1991, he led a Frontiers team into northern Iraq following the Gulf War. Bob is an ordained Presbyterian minister and author of *Ethnic Realities and the Church: Lessons from Kurdistan*. He and his wife, Jan, have three children.

TIM CAIN is the lead pastor of Kaleo Church, which he planted in 2009 in El Cajon, California. He is author of *The God of Great Reversals: The Gospel in the Book of Esther*. Tim has a passion for preaching the gospel, church planting, adoption, and feasting with the poor. He and his wife, Abbey, live in El Cajon with their two adopted children.

D. GLENN has had the pleasure of working with Arab Muslims for 14 years. He currently works with Syrian refugees in the Middle East, delivering physical aid and sowing seeds of hope. He and his wife have five children, three with them and two with the Lord.

TIM KEESEE is executive director of Frontline Missions International, an organization committed to advancing the gospel in the world's difficult places by developing sustainable platforms for work and witness. He is also the executive producer of the missions documentary series *Dispatches from the Front*. He has authored numerous books and articles on history, politics, and missions, including *Dispatches from the Front: Stories of Gospel Advance in the World's Difficult Places*. Tim is married and assisted in the ministry by his wife Debbie. They have two married children and one grandchild.

DAVID MATHIS is executive editor for desiringGod.org, pastor at Cities Church in Minneapolis/Saint Paul, and adjunct professor for Bethlehem College & Seminary. He has edited and contributed to several books and is author of *Habits of Grace: Enjoying Jesus through the Spiritual Disciplines*.

JOHN PIPER is founder and teacher of desiringGod.org and chancellor of Bethlehem College & Seminary. For more than thirty years, he served as senior pastor at Bethlehem Baptist Church, Minneapolis, Minnesota. He is the author of more than fifty books, and more than thirty years of his preaching and teaching is available, free of charge, at desiringGod.org. John and his wife, Noël, have four sons, one daughter, and twelve grandchildren.

JOE RIGNEY is assistant professor of theology and Christian worldview at Bethlehem College & Seminary. He is author of *The Things of Earth: Treasuring God by Enjoying His Gifts* and *Live Like a Narnian: Christian Discipleship in Lewis's Chronicles*. He is a pastor at Cities Church and lives in Minneapolis with his wife and two sons.

BRIAN J. TABB is associate dean for academic affairs and assistant professor of biblical studies at Bethlehem College & Seminary. He is also managing editor of *Themelios* and serves as an elder of Bethlehem Baptist Church. He and his wife, Kristin, are parents of three.

DIEUDONNÉ TAMFU is an associate pastor at Jubilee Community Church and an adjunct professor at Bethlehem College & Seminary. He and his wife, Dominique, live in Minneapolis.

STEVE TIMMIS lives in Sheffield, England, where he is the senior elder in The Crowded House. He is the executive director of Acts 29 Europe. He is married to Janet, and they have four married children, and eight grandchildren. He has co-authored a number of books with Tim Chester, including *Total Church*, as well as authoring *Gospel Centered Leadership* and *I Wish Jesus Hadn't Said That!*

Count it all joy, my brothers,
when you meet trials of various kinds.
—James 1:2

INTRODUCTION

Joy in Every Trial

David Mathis

It was a lesson in the school of hard knocks for a promising young leader.

A crowd had gathered in an urban center, ready to hear him speak. He rose to the occasion, feeling a fresh anointing of the Holy Spirit. He spoke with conviction and clarity, and found remarkable reception among the people.

But word of his explicitness about Jesus quickly made its way to the powers-that-be and ruffled their feathers. Soon they descended upon the young firebrand, and he and his ministry partner spent the night in custody before facing interrogation the following day.

Still his courage had not been in vain. They may have arrested Peter and his companion John (Acts 4:3), but "many of those who had heard the word believed, and the number of the men came to about five thousand" (Acts 4:4).

Arrest didn't sink the advance of the gospel. The two went hand in hand.

The American Anomaly

The days of gospel persecution in the United States no longer just hang on the distant horizon; they are already here, at least for some. It's beginning with the bakers, florists, and photographers. Before long, the consensus may be that faithful biblical exposition is "hate speech." Many are left wondering what trials may come in the wake of the Supreme Count's monumental decision in *Obergefell vs. Hodges*.

For 350 years, the church on American soil has enjoyed relatively little affliction for her fidelity to the Scriptures. This nation, though, is an anomaly in church history. And those days are passing, more quickly than many of us expected.

Once the most basic beliefs and morals of Christianity were taken for granted not only in the church, but in society at large. Now many of our most deeply held, once uncontroversial, claims are under full assault, within and without. Barring some change in trajectory, it may only be a matter of time before some of our leaders find themselves in custody, or under tremendous threat.

Don't Be Surprised

However, Christians should not panic. For two thousand years, this has been what it has meant to identify with Christ in the world—the normal experience of those who follow a man who was crucified. Suffering for the gospel was not just tolerated in the early church; it was expected. Peter learned the lesson in Acts 4, and again in Acts 5. Then Stephen was stoned in Acts 7. After Acts 3, only three of the book's remaining 25 chapters have no mention of persecution.

The storyline of the early church turns on opposition and oppression. This same Peter writes, "Beloved, do not be surprised at the fiery trial when it comes upon you to test you, as though something strange were happening to you" (1 Pet. 4:12).

For now, deluded by American history, we're prone to think it strange. We *are* surprised. "Give us our country back!" But angry, desperate reactions only show how out of step we are with the tenor of the New Testament. Entitlement and resentment reveal a heart foreign to the reality of "a better country, that is, a heavenly one" (Heb. 11:16).

Soon enough, though, the expectations of American Christians will necessarily adjust to what is normal for the true church in other times and places. We will increasingly realize that when we proclaim a gospel like ours, and make the sort of claims we do, the world won't typically receive it well. For Christians, it really is strange *not* to be persecuted.

Through Many Tribulations

Jesus said as much. "'A servant is not greater than his master.' If they persecuted me, they *will* also persecute you" (John 15:20). Paul picks up the refrain. "Indeed, all who desire to live a godly life in Christ Jesus *will* be persecuted" (2 Tim. 3:12). The Scriptures seem to suggest we should be more concerned if we're not being persecuted, than if we are.

Embracing persecution for the sake of the gospel is Christianity 101. How did Paul and Barnabas minister to fledgling churches? "They returned to Lystra and to Iconium and to Antioch, strengthening the souls of the disciples, encouraging them to continue in the faith, and saying that *through many tribulations we must enter the kingdom of God*" (Acts 14:21–22). It is a sobering word, but not a cause for despair.

ARREST AND ADVANCE, TOGETHER

To say we will suffer opposition is not to say that the spread of the gospel will be stymied. In fact, what we learn from Peter and John in Acts 4:3–4, and from the life of the apostle Paul, and from Jesus himself, is that arrest and advance go together in God's invincible story.

The same is true today, and will be tomorrow. We will find that our newfound opposition and affliction, while being difficult and painful, is a good and fruitful phenomenon. It will be more and more like the first century, when the gospel was attacked on every side, and spread like wildfire.

Paul describes this powerfully from a prison cell in Rome. Look for the irony.

> I want you to know, brothers, that what has happened to me has really served to advance the gospel, so that it has become known throughout the whole imperial guard and to all the rest that my imprisonment is for Christ. And most of the brothers, having become confident in the Lord by my imprisonment, are much more bold to speak the word without fear. (Phil. 1:12–14)

You can't arrest the gospel. In fact, when you imprison one whose words and life boldly declare the good news of Jesus, you only help it grow and spread. You may shackle the feet of the messenger, but his message will run. "Remember Jesus Christ, risen from the dead, the offspring of David, as preached in my gospel, for which I am suffering, bound with chains as a criminal. But the word of God is not bound!" (2 Tim. 2:8–9).

AFFLICTION JOYFULLY ACCEPTED

But our message will not run if we go kicking and screaming. It is not the grumblers and complainers who shine as lights in the midst of a crooked and perverse generation (Phil. 2:14–15). Rather, it is those who embrace suffering for the name of Jesus with joy.

> Rejoice insofar as you share Christ's sufferings, that you may also rejoice and be glad when his glory is revealed. If you are insulted for the name of Christ, you are blessed, because the Spirit of glory and of God rests upon you. (1 Pet. 4:13–14)

Christians are not a dour people, even in the darkness of a dungeon. We don't whine and bellyache as our society lines up against our convictions. We plead. We grieve. But beneath it all, we have untouchable strongholds of joy. Even in the worst, most inconvenient, most lonely days, we rejoice. The suffering days are good days for gospel advance. We have great cause to be optimistic about our good news, to "joyfully accept" prison and the plundering of our possessions and even our freedoms. After all, they can take our civil liberties, garnish our wages, and smear our names, but they cannot take our Treasure, who is "a better possession and an abiding one" (Heb. 10:34).

And so we are not surprised. We do not retreat. Instead, grounded in God's eternal promises, armed with joy in him, and assured of victory in the end, we ready ourselves for whatever opposition comes. Perhaps one day it will be said of us,

> You endured a hard struggle with sufferings, sometimes being publicly exposed to reproach and affliction, and sometimes being partners with those so treated. For you had compassion on those in prison, and you joyfully accepted the plundering of your property, since you knew that you yourselves had a better possession and an abiding one. (Heb. 10:32–34)

Navigating the New America

In the chapters that follow, a diverse team of contributors, representing six continents, joins forces to help American Christians get ready for the insults, trials, opposition, and even persecution that may lie ahead. We pray it makes for a soul-strengthening blend of biblical exposition and inspiring anecdotes from the persecuted church throughout history and around the world.

After John Piper's opening charge to be "winsome weirdos" to a society in which we find ourselves increasingly alien, Brian Tabb and Joe Rigney send out roots down deep with the story of the early church in the Book of Acts. If there were any question whether the church could thrive under trial, the story of the early church will set the record straight. And few things will put ballast in the boat of the twenty-first-century American church like reckoning in depth and detail with the trials and persecutions of those first believers—and the indispensible role resistance served in the advance of the gospel.

Chapters 4–7, then, form the heart of the book. Four contributors, representing four nations, feed our faith with stories of Christian endurance, with joy, under the throes of persecution. Dieudonné Tamfu, from Cameroon, bridges the gap from the post-apostolic fathers all the way down to the threat of Boko Haram in Africa today. Steve Timmis, from the United Kingdom, gives us a glimpse not only into what may be looming in his post-Christian nation, but sobers us with stories from his ministry among the persecuted underground church in the 1980s Soviet Union. In chapter 6, Tim Keesee opens windows for us into places like Pakistan, the Middle East, and North Africa where the doors are "closed" to gospel witness—and suffering for the faith is the norm for Christians. D. Glenn, then, who works among Syrian refugees fleeing the horrors of isis, invites us into "The Fellowship of the Suffering."

The final two chapters take us for what may seem like a surprising turn. In chapter 8, Tim Cain, church planter among the poor in San Diego, prepares us for the opposition that will come from within. The Enemy loves to deplete our strength, and weaken our witness, by sowing seeds of strife among Christians. Opposition from without may rally us and draw us together, but it won't be long until there is internal tension. Then what will we do?

In chapter 9, Bob Blincoe puts the call to face our fiery trials in the States in perspective by renewing our call to complete the Commission in the hardest places on the planet. Will opposition at home tempt us to circle our North American wagons, or will it inspire resilience enough to send even our own sons and daughters to exceedingly more difficult places to answer Jesus's call?

Finally, Piper sounds the last note from 1 Peter 3:15. We are to be always "prepared to make a defense to anyone who asks you for a reason for the hope that is in you." Are unbelievers asking about our hope? What will it take to have them asking in the new America?

Our prayer is that God would be pleased to use these short and simple chapters to stir your faith and make you one of the happy Christians who will be undaunted in the coming days, and have the wherewithal to see that these are great days to be alive, for the sake of gospel advance and the fame of Jesus. May he steady your ship for the storms to come.

*They are surprised when you do not join them
in the same flood of debauchery,
and they malign you.*
−1 Peter 4:4

WINSOME WEIRDOS

A Serious Call for a Special Breed

John Piper

According to the apostle Peter's first letter, labeling Christians as "winsome weirdos" is not only linguistically alliterative; it is also exegetically accurate. The implications for our cultural moment in America are crucial. I have especially in mind 1 Peter 4:3–4:

> The time that is past suffices for doing what the Gentiles want to do, living in sensuality, passions, drunkenness, orgies, drinking parties, and lawless idolatry. With respect to this they are surprised when you do not join them in the same flood of debauchery, and they malign you.

Two statements stand out: "they are *surprised*," and "they *malign* you."

The word here for "surprised" (Greek *xenizontai*) is translated "strange things" in Acts 17:20 ("You *bring some strange* things to our ears"). It's built on the word for *strange, foreign,* or *unfamiliar* (*xenos*).

Eight verses later, both the verb (*xenizesthe*) and the adjective (*xenou*) forms are used to describe the persecution of Christians: "Beloved, do not be *surprised* at the fiery trial when it comes upon you to test you, as though something *strange* were happening to you" (1 Pet. 4:12). We might paraphrase it by saying: "Don't think it strange (4:12) when they think you are strange (4:4)."

Sojourners and Exiles

The first sparks of the "fiery trial" are already flying as Peter writes. They include the "maligning" of Christians in verse 4. The word translated "malign" is *blasphemeo*—from which we get our English word *blaspheme*. The Greek dictionary defines it as, "slander, revile, defame, speak irreverently/impiously/disrespectfully of or about."

What, then, is the situation as a whole?

Peter has already identified the Christians as "elect *exiles*" (1 Pet. 1:1), whom he urges "as *sojourners and exiles* to abstain from the passions of the flesh, which wage war against your soul" (1 Pet. 2:11). The entire Christian life is "the time of your *exile*" (1 Pet. 1:17). In other words, we are "strangers (*xenoi*) and exiles on the earth" (Heb. 11:13).

The implication of this "foreign" status of Christians among the cultures of the world is that the new birth (1 Pet. 1:3, 23) has given us new desires (1 Pet. 1:14; 2:2) that no longer match "what the Gentiles want to do" (1 Pet. 4:3). The result is a disruption of whom we literally "run with" (v. 4). And this disruption causes our associates to be "surprised." That is, they think it "strange" that we are not running with them into the same "sensuality, passions, drunkenness, orgies, drinking parties, and lawless idolatry" (1 Pet. 4:3).

Weirdos

This reaction to our new *strangeness* is so strong that they "malign" (*blaphemountes*) us. This is where I see the idea of "weirdo." Their response to our "strangeness" is not mild or respectful. It is strong and severe. The word "malign" does *not* mean they say: "We all have our preferences, and we can live and let live with mutual respect." No. "Malign," together with "see as strange," means they are using strong language to insult the Christians. The label "weirdo" would be among the more mild results of our new way of life.

Other results of Christians becoming culturally alien "weirdos," who are out of step with "what the Gentiles want to do" (1 Pet. 4:3), include being "reviled" (1 Pet. 3:9, 16), being called "evildoers" (1 Pet. 2:12), "suffering" (1 Pet. 3:14, 17–18), and being "beaten" (1 Pet. 2:20).

Weirdness Embraced

What makes this situation remarkable is that the apostle Peter calls us to embrace it, but then to do so many good deeds, that at least some of our detractors are won over, and even glorify God because of our lives. Not because we become less "weird," but because we are *more* than weird.

First, notice that our "weirdness" is *called for* by Peter, and *embraced* by us. He says we are to "live for the rest of the time in the flesh no longer for human passions but for the will of God. For the time that is past suffices for doing what the Gentiles want to do" (1 Pet. 4:2–3). In other words, we are to choose to march out of step with a society that is driven by "human passions," and in step with the "will of God." Weirdness called for. Chosen. Embraced.

WINSOME WEIRDNESS

But, second, notice that just as prominent in this book is the call to be so busy with good deeds that those who malign us are "silenced," "shamed," and "converted."

> This is the will of God, that by doing good you should put *to silence the ignorance* of foolish people. (1 Pet. 2:15)

> [Have] a good conscience, so that, when you are slandered, those who revile your good behavior in Christ may be *put to shame*. (1 Pet. 3:16)

> Keep your conduct among the Gentiles honorable, so that when they speak against you as evildoers, they may see your good deeds and *glorify God* on the day of visitation. (1 Pet. 2:12)

Our aim in filling our lives with "good deeds" is that

- ignorant and foolish criticism of Christians would be revealed and silenced,
- slanderous reviling of Christians would be put to shame, and
- best of all, calling Christians "evildoers" would be converted into calling God glorious.

That is where I get the word "winsome."

In Step and Out of Step

What is striking and paradoxical in 1 Peter is the mandate that Christians are to be *both* out of step with their culture, *and* compelling in the culture. We are to be weird and winsome.

The key in 1 Peter is that the inevitable moral weirdness that arises from replacing "human passions" with the "will of God" (1 Pet. 4:2), and replacing "passions of former ignorance" (1 Pet. 1:14) with joy in Christ and his ways (1 Pet. 1:6, 8; 2:3; 4:13), is matched with a Christian zeal for "good deeds" (1 Pet. 2:15, 20; 3:6, 9, 11, 13, 14, 17; 4:19). Perhaps Peter's strongest statement of this zeal is that we are to be "zealous for the good" (1 Pet. 3:13).

And it needs to be stressed that "good deeds" are not merely the avoidance of bad behavior. (That avoidance is crucial. It is essential throughout 1 Peter. That is why we are maligned as "weirdos.") But "good deeds" are the proactive efforts to "bless" those who revile us (3:9).

Of course, there are many things Christians regard as *good* which society will call *evil*. That is what Peter says: "They speak against you as evildoers" (1 Pet. 2:12). But right alongside of that recognition, Peter presses us: "that they may see your good deeds and glorify God on the day of visitation" (1 Pet. 2:12). These are deeds that, if God wills, even the hostile culture will see as good.

The Relevance for the New America

What makes this so relevant today is that American culture is increasingly out of step with the way of life that the Bible calls "how you ought to walk and to please God" (1

Thess. 4:1). Proposals about how Christians should respond to this situation include (as a recent symposium in *Christianity Today* illustrates[1]), the Benedict Option (Rod Dreher), the Wilberforce Option (Peter Wehner and Michael Gerson), and the Dr. King Option (Gabriel Salguero). It seems to me that all of these options embody aspects of the response to culture that are needed in our day: ongoing engagement, creating alternative communities, readiness to surrender dominance.

What the apostle Peter contributes to this debate, among other things, is this: Baby Boomers (like me) who grew up with an assumed overlap between Christian morality and cultural expectations, and Millennials, who desperately want to be hip and cool, must both joyfully embrace the calling to be *weirdos*. It is not our culture. And we are not cool.

And with just as much resolve and joy, we must set our faces to be *winsome*. Not by cowering before the slander, or desperately trying to avoid being maligned, but by getting up every morning dreaming of what new good deeds can be done today. What fresh way can I "bless" my enemies (1 Pet. 3:9) or anyone in need? This may be as simple as a genuine conversation with the woman panhandling at the corner of 11th Avenue and 17th Street. Or it may be creating a ministry as huge as World Vision, Samaritan's Purse, or Food for the Hungry.

The apostle Peter is calling for a special breed. Not the kind of conservative who gives all his energy to em-

---

1. Michael Gerson and Peter Wehner, "How Christians Can Flourish in a Same-Sex-Marriage World," November 2, 2015. Accessed online at http://www.christianitytoday.com/ct/2015/november/how-christians-can-flourish-in-same-sex-marriage-world-cult.html.

bracing and defending his weirdo status. And not the kind of liberal who will embrace any compromise necessary to avoid being a weirdo. But rather a breed that is courageous enough to be joyfully weird, and compassionate enough to be "zealous for what is good" (1 Pet. 3:13).

*"These men who have turned the world
upside down have come here also."*
−Acts 17:6

2

TURNING THE WORLD UPSIDE DOWN

Gospel Advance against All Odds

Brian J. Tabb

Jesus tells his disciples to get ready for trouble. He sets his face to go to Jerusalem, the city that persecutes the prophets, and embraces God's mysterious plan for the Son to suffer many things and die for his people (Luke 9:22, 51). Jesus reminds them that he will suffer, and so will his disciples.

> Blessed are you when people hate you and when they exclude you and revile you and spurn your name as evil, on account of the Son of Man! Rejoice in that day, and leap for joy, for behold, your reward is great in heaven; for so their fathers did to the prophets. (Luke 6:22–23)

> If anyone would come after me, let him deny himself and take up his cross daily and follow me. (Luke 9:23)

> And when they bring you before the synagogues and the rulers and the authorities, do not be

anxious about how you should defend yourself
or what you should say, for the Holy Spirit will
teach you in that very hour what you ought to
say. (Luke 12:11–12)

They will lay their hands on you and persecute
you, delivering you up to the synagogues and
prisons, and you will be brought before kings
and governors for my name's sake. This will be
your opportunity to bear witness. . . . You will
be delivered up even by parents and brothers
and relatives and friends, and some of you they
will put to death. You will be hated by all for
my name's sake. But not a hair of your head will
perish. (Luke 21:12–18)

These sober warnings and exhortations set the stage for
how Jesus's disciples will carry out his mission in the
book of Acts. The risen Lord Jesus fulfills God's ancient
promises and establishes his kingdom among all nations,
and he does this *through* his Spirit-empowered, suffering
people.[2] Ordinary people "turned the world upside down"
as they followed their suffering, risen King (Acts 17:6–7).
Acts presents us with at least five important truths about
suffering.[3]

---

2. For a similar explanation of the message of Acts, see Alan J. Thomp-
   son, *The Acts of the Risen Lord Jesus: Luke's Account of God's Unfolding
   Plan*, New Studies in Biblical Theology 27 (Downers Grove, IL:
   InterVarsity Press, 2011), 29–67.
3. For a fuller treatment of suffering in Acts, see Brian J. Tabb, "Salvation, Spreading, and Suffering: God's Unfolding Plan in Luke-Acts,"
   JETS 58 (2015): 43–61.

1. The Son's Suffering Secures Our Salvation

Peter declares that there is "forgiveness of sins" and "salvation in no other name" than that of Jesus, the crucified and exalted Lord and Messiah (Acts 2:38; 4:12). Other New Testament authors explain more explicitly *how* Jesus's righteous suffering and death secure atonement for sin, justification, and reconciliation to God.[4] Luke and Acts stress *that* Jesus suffered, died, and rose on the third day to fulfill God's ancient promises and secure salvation and forgiveness of sins for all nations.[5] At his final Passover meal Jesus tells his disciples, "This is my body, which is given *for you*. Do this in remembrance of me. . . . This cup that is poured out *for you* is the new covenant in my blood" (Luke 22:19–20).

Central to the "new covenant" that Jeremiah announced is a restored relationship between God and his people based upon God's glorious promise to forgive sins (Jer. 31:31, 34). So Jesus explains after his resurrection, "Thus it is written, that the Messiah should suffer and on the third day rise from the dead, and that repentance and forgiveness of sins should be proclaimed in his name to all nations, beginning from Jerusalem" (Luke 24:46–47). Through his unjust suffering and shed blood on the cross, Jesus fulfills Scripture and redeems his new covenant people, the church (Acts 20:28).

---

4. For example, Matthew 20:28; Romans 5:6–11; Hebrews 2:9–10; 1 Peter 3:18. See the excellent treatment in John Piper, *Fifty Reasons Why Jesus Came to Die* (Wheaton, IL: Crossway, 2006).

5. Cf. Darrell L. Bock, *A Theology of Luke and Acts*, Biblical Theology of the New Testament (Grand Rapids: Zondervan, 2012), 253.

2. Jesus's Witnesses Suffer Like Their Lord and for His Name

Jesus promises that persecutions and trials will be his disciples' "opportunity to bear witness" (Luke 21:13), and Acts records how that happens for the Twelve and other leaders like Stephen and Paul.[6] Suffering for the gospel does not disqualify these people but actually confirms that they are genuine leaders who follow and proclaim a suffering, risen Lord. Acts 4–5 confirms that the Twelve are God's appointed leaders in at least five ways.

- The same Jewish leaders that condemned Jesus and called for his crucifixion persecute his apostles.[7]

- These opponents recognize the apostles' connection to Jesus precisely when they boldly testify to the truth in the face of adversity (Acts 4:8, 13–14; cf. Luke 21:15).

- The apostles who suffer demonstrate that they obey God not people, while the Jewish leaders who persecute them stand dangerously opposed to God and his Messiah (Acts 5:29–32).[8]

---

6. I summarize how Acts fulfills Jesus's predictions of persecution and proclamation in "Salvation, Spreading, and Suffering," 54.
7. Luke 22:66; 23:13; 24:20; Acts 4:5–6; 5:28–29. Scott S. Cunningham lists parallels between Jesus and the apostles in *"Through Many Tribulations": The Theology of Persecution in Luke-Acts*, JSNTSup 142 (Sheffield: Sheffield Academic, 1997), 195–96.
8. Similarly, the risen Jesus asks Saul, "Why are you persecuting me?" (Acts 9:4).

- The apostles are beaten just like their Master (Acts 5:40; Luke 22:63), and the church interprets threats against the apostles as extending or continuing the opposition to their Lord (Acts 4:27–28).

- The apostles experience God's presence and power in times of suffering (Acts 4:16, 30). God miraculously delivers the apostles from prison, thwarting their opponents' efforts to muzzle the Messiah's messengers (5:19–25).[9]

Similarly, in Acts 6–7 Stephen's persecution fulfills Jesus's predictions and follows the pattern of Jesus's passion. Stephen's opponents cannot withstand his Spirit-filled wisdom, just as Jesus said (Acts 6:10; Luke 21:15). Stephen, like Jesus, appears before the Jewish council (Luke 22:66; Acts 6:12, 15), is maligned by false witnesses (Mark 14:56–58; Acts 6:13–14), is charged with blasphemy (Mark 14:64; Acts 6:11; cf. 7:58), and cries with a loud voice when he dies (Luke 23:46; Acts 7:60). Additionally, Stephen's last words in Acts 7:56–60 recall sayings of Jesus during his passion (Luke 22:69; 23:34, 46), and Stephen addresses his prayers to his risen, vindicated Lord.

Jesus declares that Saul "must suffer for the sake of my name" (Acts 9:16), and soon the Jews oppose and even try to kill their former leader Saul when he boldly preaches about Jesus (9:23, 29), which confirms to Ananias and other fearful, persecuted believers that this former persecutor is indeed a true disciple and witness of Jesus. Later, Paul declares to the Ephesian elders that he fully embraces his

---

9. See also Acts 12:6–11 and 16:25–28.

calling "to testify to the gospel of the grace of God," while enduring "imprisonment and afflictions" in every city (Acts 20:23–24). Like Jesus, Paul sets his face to go to Jerusalem and declares that he is ready to suffer and even die for Jesus's name (Acts 21:13).

3. Suffering Is Central to Spreading the Gospel

Acts 1:8 clearly summarizes the disciples' mission between Jesus's exaltation and return: "You will receive power when the Holy Spirit has come upon you, and you will be my witnesses in Jerusalem and in all Judea and Samaria, and to the end of the earth." Jesus pours out the Spirit on the day of Pentecost, and Peter and the other apostles start preaching the gospel with boldness and clarity, beginning in Jerusalem (Acts 2:1–40). Many who hear this message believe and are baptized (Acts 2:41), but opposition begins to mount. First, Jewish leaders arrest, imprison, and interrogate Peter and John after they heal a lame man at the temple (Acts 4:1–22). Then the high priest and his party arrest all the apostles out of jealousy. They beat the apostles and warn them to stop speaking about Jesus, but these adversaries cannot quench their joy or thwart their mission in Jerusalem (Acts 5:40–42; 6:7).

The opposition to the church reaches a tipping point with Stephen when an angry mob arrests, questions, and stones him to death (Acts 6:12; 7:54–60). His martyrdom unleashes "a great persecution against the church in Jerusalem," and believers scatter throughout Judea and Samaria as Saul ravaged the church (Acts 8:1–3). Remarkably, this scattering catalyzes increased mission beyond Jerusalem since "those who were scattered went about preaching the word" (Acts 8:4). Philip brings the gospel to Samaria (8:4–25), fulfilling Jesus's promise in Acts 1:8. Furthermore, the believers who scattered because enemies persecuted them "traveled as far as Phoenicia and Cyprus and Antioch," where they began to evangelize Gentiles (Acts 11:19–21). Then Barnabas brings Saul (later Paul)—the very one who persecuted believers and scattered them from Jerusalem—to teach these new believers in Antioch (Acts 11:25–27).

Next, Paul and Barnabas proclaim the gospel in Pisidian Antioch, and jealous Jewish leaders oppose them. Paul and Barnabas boldly declare they are turning to the Gentiles to obey what the Lord has commanded (from Isa. 49:6): "Bring salvation to the end of the earth" (Acts 13:46–47), again explicitly recalling Acts 1:8. In city after city, Paul faces "imprisonment and afflictions" (Acts 20:23), but God's word continues to go forth. In fact, it is as a prisoner that Paul boldly proclaims the gospel before King Agrippa (Acts 26:1–29)—fulfilling Jesus's words in Acts 9:15–16. Luke's narrative ends with Paul under house arrest in Rome, "proclaiming the kingdom of God and teaching about the Lord Jesus Christ with all boldness and without hindrance" (Acts 28:31). Thus, God consistently appoints adversity and opposition to advance Jesus's mission in Jerusalem, Judea and Samaria, and unto the ends of the earth.

4. Suffering and Injustice Will Cease When God's Kingdom Comes in Its Fullness

In Acts 14:22, Paul and Barnabas strengthen and encourage disciples to continue in the faith "saying that through many tribulations we must enter the kingdom of God." Three truths follow from this important verse. First, *all* believers, not merely apostles or missionaries, should expect present suffering while we await future glory. Second, God often calls leaders to suffer well as an example for others to follow. The first person "we" in Acts 14:22 includes the missionaries and their hearers—believers in Lystra, Iconium, and Antioch. The last time Paul came to Lystra, he was stoned, dragged out of the city, and left for dead (v. 19). Paul experiences difficult, painful trials, as Jesus promised that he would (Acts 9:16), and in Acts 14 he faithfully suffers in the way he calls other Christians to suffer. Third, tribulations are necessary, but they are a means and not an end in themselves. Jesus suffered and then entered into glory (Luke 24:26), and his followers who suffer now should confidently expect to enter into glory when God's kingdom comes in its fullness.

God's people endure suffering and trouble now, but we look forward to "the time for restoring all the things about which God spoke by the mouth of his holy prophets long ago" (Acts 3:21). Jesus has risen from the dead, ascended to his heavenly throne, and poured out the Holy Spirit in the last days (Acts 2:32–33). Paul proclaims that the Messiah was "the first to rise from the dead" (Acts 26:23), which means that Jesus's resurrection already guarantees the future resurrection of his people in the future. The resurrection also means that God has begun to fulfill his promises to restore all things. In Acts 3–4, a lame beggar is healed and saved by the name of Jesus, which recalls God's promise to come and save his people, when the lame will "leap like a deer" (Isa. 35:4–6). David Peterson explains,

In raising him [Jesus] from the dead, God began the great process of renewal and restoration that will culminate in a transformed creation and the general resurrection of all believers to eternal life.... What happened to the crippled man was an anticipation of the glory to come, but also a sign of the present, heavenly authority of the exalted Christ to save in the ultimate sense.[10]

5. SUFFERING BELIEVERS SHOULD PRAY, BEAR WITNESS, AND REJOICE

Believers in Acts consistently respond to suffering and trouble by praying, just as Jesus taught in Luke 6:28. Acts 4:24–30 models how to pray in times of persecution:

> Sovereign Lord, who made the heaven and the earth and the sea and everything in them, who through the mouth of our father David, your servant, said by the Holy Spirit, "Why did the Gentiles rage, and the peoples plot in vain? The kings of the earth set themselves, and the rulers were gathered together, against the Lord and against his Anointed"—for truly in this city there were gathered together against your holy servant Jesus, whom you anointed, both Herod and Pontius Pilate, along with the Gentiles and the peoples of Israel, to do whatever your hand and your plan had predestined to take place. And now, Lord, look upon their threats and grant to your servants to continue to speak your word with all boldness, while you stretch out your hand

---

10. David G. Peterson, *The Acts of the Apostles*, Pillar New Testament Commentary (Grand Rapids: Eerdmans, 2009), 190.

to heal, and signs and wonders are performed
through the name of your holy servant Jesus.

These believers affirm God's sovereign power and understand that Jesus and the apostles suffer according to God's
plan as Scripture reveals (Psalm 2:1–2). Further, they do not
pray that God would deliver them *from* suffering, but that
he would help them to go on speaking the word boldly *in*
times of suffering. God answers this prayer in Acts 4:31:
"they were all filled with the Holy Spirit and continued to
speak the word of God with boldness."

Leaders throughout Acts—especially Peter, Stephen,
and Paul—boldly preach in times of adversity, just as Jesus
said in Luke 21:12–15. Additionally, Acts 5:41 says that the
apostles "left the presence of the council, rejoicing that
they were counted worthy to suffer dishonor for the name."
Similarly, after enemies beat them with rods and locked
them up in prison without any fair trial or due process,
Paul and Silas respond by praying and singing hymns to
God (Acts 16:25). Christians in Acts rejoice and sing when
suffering comes because their hope is not fixed on human
approval or comfortable circumstances but on a surpass-
ingly great heavenly reward (Luke 6:23).

Turn the World Upside Down

Acts recounts how a group of joyful, gospel-speaking,
suffering followers of King Jesus "turned the world upside
down" (Acts 17:6–7). They feared God more than people.
They did not doubt God in suffering, but kept speaking
about their King. They spoke with the Spirit's power, not
human wisdom. They were shamefully treated and yet

rejoiced. They filled the prison with singing. They prayed for boldness, not comfort. They maintained hope in adversity because they believed in the resurrection. They were scattered through persecution, but stayed focused on God's mission. They knew that "through many tribulations we must enter the kingdom of God" (Acts 14:22).

"We strictly charged you not to teach in this name, yet here you have filled Jerusalem with your teaching."
–Acts 5:28

3

A STRANGE AND SURPRISING TRIUMPH

How Early-Church Suffering Shapes the Christian Imagination

Joe Rigney

Man is a story-telling animal. As individuals, as families, as churches, as communities, as nations, we tell ourselves stories in order to make sense of where we've come from and where we're going and what our role in the story is.

One of our tasks as Christians is to learn to read our stories in light of the biblical story: both the Big Story of God's mission to rescue the world from sin and death through Jesus and the smaller stories within the Big Story that shed light on our circumstances. To do this, we must recover a Scripture-shaped imagination, one that is trained to run in biblical ruts, formed and molded by the word of God. This means reading the narratives of Scripture as God intended them to be read—as authoritative records of God's works in history. As we read them, we take note of the stories that God likes to tell, knowing that, while history may not repeat itself, it does rhyme.

The Bible is filled with good stories like this—stories with characters, conflict, and triumph over adversity. The Book of Acts is one such story. Or rather, it is one such story that is filled with many smaller stories, chapters in the great Story of God. The present chapter will explore one of these chapters—the story of the early church in Jerusalem, recorded for us in Acts 1–7. Space constraints will limit application to our own day; my hope is that in reading and recognizing the patterns in these chapters, your mind will be instructed in the ways of our God, your imagination will be formed by his patterns, and your heart will be moved to worship.

We begin with the main characters in this section of Acts. There are four groups of them: 1) the apostles (the leaders of the fledgling church); 2) the believers (those who have embraced the risen Jesus as the Messiah); 3) the Jewish crowds (among whom the apostles are ministering and preaching); and 4) the Sanhedrin (the Jewish leaders who oppose the new Jesus movement). The first seven chapters of Acts follow these four groups as they collide with one another again and again.

Escalating Conflict

Collision is the word for it. Conflict abounds in these chapters, with the apostles and the Jewish leaders publicly colliding three times (4:1–22; 5:17–41; 6:8–7:60; for purposes of this chapter, I'm treating Stephen as an apostle, even though technically he was not). The cause of these collisions is obvious: The Sanhedrin opposes the apostolic testimony. What's not so obvious is that their opposition *escalates* over the first seven chapters, and this escalating opposition is one of the key ways that Acts ought to shape our imaginations. We can recognize this escalation in three ways:

- the *motive* for arresting the apostles
- the *response* to the apostolic witness
- the *resolution* to the tense situation

In terms of motive, we move from theological annoyance (Acts 4) to envy and jealousy (Acts 5) to outright hatred and slander (Acts 6–7). In the first collision, the Sadducees arrest Peter and John because they were "greatly annoyed because they were teaching the people and proclaiming in Jesus the resurrection from the dead" (Acts 4:2; Sadducees, you'll remember, didn't believe in the resurrection, Acts 23:6–8). In the second collision, the Sadducees, "filled with jealousy," arrested the apostles (Acts 5:17). Finally, unable to withstand Stephen's wisdom, they stir up slander and lies against him in order to have a pretense for his arrest (Acts 6:10–14).

In terms of the Sanhedrin's response, we move from amazement (Acts 4) to barely controlled anger (Acts 5) to uncontrollable rage (Acts 7). In each collision, the apostles stand before the council and give a defense. And in each case, the response of the Jewish leaders escalates. After the apostolic testimony in Acts 4, the leaders are "astonished" at the boldness of the apostles (verse 13). They can't believe that uneducated fishermen could understand the Scriptures with such insight. In the second collision, Peter and the apostles stand firm under scrutiny, and their testimony is met with barely controlled rage (they want to kill the apostles, but Gamaliel is able to calm them down, 5:33–40). In the final encounter, Stephen's sermon sends them into a frenzy of teeth-grinding rage (7:54).

Finally, in terms of resolution, we move from verbal warning (Acts 4) to violent warning (Acts 5) to murder by mob (Acts 7). In the first encounter, after the Jewish leaders get over their amazement, they release Peter and John with a verbal warning ("Don't preach in this name anymore," 4:18). After the second, they add a beating to their warning ("We already told you once," 5:40). And the final encounter ends with the stoning of Stephen.

The Roots of Rising Opposition

What accounts for this rising conflict? Why does the hostility and violence intensify in this way? We see two main causes. First is the phenomenal growth of the church. Acts 1 begins with a small community of about 120 people (1:15). By the end of Acts 2, that number has jumped by three thousand souls (2:41), with more added every day (2:47). By Acts 4, the church has grown to include five thousand men (4:4). And in Acts 5:14, we're told that "more than ever believers were added to the Lord, multitudes of both men and women." In light of this growth, it's no surprise that the Jewish leaders move from viewing the apostles with annoyance to being filled with envy and jealousy. They are losing their grip on the Jewish crowds, as the ranks of the church swell with people from all walks of life.

The second cause of the escalation is the apostolic boldness. It is this boldness that initially astonished the Sanhedrin in Acts 4:13. But what do we mean by boldness? Boldness in the Bible is not swagger; it's not machismo and angry bravado. The only people who are filled with anger in these chapters are the Sanhedrin. Instead, Christian boldness is courage and clarity about Jesus and sin. Christian boldness doesn't muddle the message; that would be confusion, not clarity. And Christian boldness doesn't muzzle the message; that would be cowardice, not courage.

We see both elements in Acts 5:27–32.

> The high priest questioned them, saying, "We strictly charged you not to teach in this name, yet here you have filled Jerusalem with your teaching, and you intend to bring this man's blood upon us." But Peter and the apostles answered, "We must obey God rather than men. The God of our fathers raised Jesus, whom you killed by hanging him on a tree. God exalted him at his right hand as Leader and Savior, to give repentance to Israel and forgiveness of sins. And we are witnesses to these things, and so is the Holy Spirit, whom God has given to those who obey him."

"You have filled Jerusalem with your teaching." What teaching? The teaching about the resurrection of Jesus. The apostles are preaching the lordship of the risen Jesus. "God exalted him at his right hand as Leader and Savior, to give repentance to Israel and forgiveness of sins." That's what every sermon in Acts is about. God raised Jesus. God exalted Jesus. Jesus is Savior. Jesus is Lord. Jesus forgives sins. There is no other name by which we can be saved. This is the message the apostles preach in defiance of the Sanhedrin's threats. They are determined to fill Jerusalem with the good news about who Jesus is and what God has done through him.

But it's not simply that they boldly preach about who Jesus is and what he's done. They also preach clearly and courageously about sin, and in particular the sin of betraying, rejecting, denying, and murdering Jesus. "You intend to bring this man's blood upon us. You're trying to blame us for killing him" (Acts 5:28). "That's exactly right," responds Peter. "You killed him by hanging him on a tree" (5:30). It's remarkable how often the apostles strike this note, in Jerusalem no less, only a few months removed from the crucifixion itself. This is very fresh, and yet the apostles make it a repeated and central note in their preaching, both to the crowds and to the Jewish leaders.

> "This Jesus, delivered up according to the definite plan and foreknowledge of God, *you crucified and killed by the hands of lawless men*." (Acts 2:23)

> "God has made him both Lord and Christ, this Jesus *whom you crucified*." (Acts 2:36)

> "The God of Abraham, the God of Isaac, and the God of Jacob, the God of our fathers, glorified his servant Jesus, whom *you delivered over and denied* in the presence of Pilate, when he had decided to release him. But *you denied the Holy and Righteous One*, and asked for a murderer to be granted to you, and *you killed the Author of life*, whom God raised from the dead. To this we are witnesses." (Acts 3:13–15)

> "By the name of Jesus Christ of Nazareth, *whom you crucified*, whom God raised from the dead. . . . This Jesus is the stone that was *rejected by you*, the builders." (Acts 4:10–11)

And this clarity and courage about the particular sin of killing Jesus is one part of the larger apostolic clarity about all sin and the need to repent.

> "Repent and be baptized every one of you in the name of Jesus Christ for the forgiveness of your sins, and you will receive the gift of the Holy Spirit. . . . Save yourselves from this crooked generation." (Acts 2:38, 40)

> "Repent therefore, and turn back, that your sins may be blotted out. . ." (Acts 3:19)

> "God, having raised up his servant, sent him to you first, to bless you *by turning every one of you from your wickedness.*" (Acts 3:26)

"Every one of you from *your* wickedness." Not your neighbor's wickedness. Not the wickedness of those people over there. *Your* wickedness. This is Christian boldness—clearly and courageously testifying to the resurrection of Jesus and the need to repent, both in general and in the specific ways that we have rebelled against God. And such boldness, which leads to the explosive growth of the church, accounts for the escalating hostility to the apostles on the part of the Jewish leaders.

Where Boldness Comes From

It's not enough to know *that* the apostles were bold in the face of threats; we must press in to see *where this boldness came from.* The first and most important source of boldness is the Holy Spirit. The apostles are bold because they ask God to make them bold. "Lord, look upon their threats and grant to your servants to continue to speak your word with all boldness.... And when they had prayed, the place in which they were gathered together was shaken, and they were all filled with the Holy Spirit and continued to speak the word of God with boldness" (Acts 4:29, 31).

But the Holy Spirit doesn't operate in a vacuum. He uses means. And the most obvious means in these chapters is the formation of the church. In fact, the early chapters of Acts have a rhythm: Luke moves between focusing on the internal workings of the church to focusing on the church's witness in the world. Inward and outward, inward and outward, with each outward movement including greater growth and greater opposition. One reason for this rhythm is to show the kind of community that produces Christian boldness. Christian boldness emerges from a *resilient* community, united in one heart and soul around the testimony of the resurrection. This is why the inward focus of Acts 2:42–47 and 4:32–37 is so crucial. A resilient community is a community of grace, in which believers steward their resources to meet the needs of others. Goods are held in common, not in some quasi-socialistic fashion, but in the sense that there is a deep and abiding commitment to the proposition, "There will be no needy person among us. We will sacrifice our wealth in service to the household of faith" (4:32–35).

So great power in preaching the resurrection leads to great grace in meeting needs, particularly in the church. But it's clear in Acts 1–7 that generosity doesn't stop at the doors of the church. Grace spills over the banks of God's household and meets the needs of outsiders. Christians are committed to seeking the good of the city. Thus, the apostles are out among the people, healing and restoring those who were broken (3:1–10; 5:12–16). What's more, the early chapters of Acts show us the necessity of holiness and integrity. A bold church is a *holy* church. Whenever there is a genuine work of God, it won't be five minutes before counterfeits show up, aping generosity in order to win fame and renown (5:1–11). Thus, not only must a boldness-producing community be filled with generosity and sacrifice; it must be holy, upright, and honest. As Ananias and Sapphira demonstrate, we cannot lie to God and expect his blessing (5:4–5). God is not mocked; he is a consuming fire, and insists that we live in holy fear before him.

So where does Christian boldness come from? It comes from God the Father, who fills us with the Holy Spirit. The Spirit gathers a people around the preaching of the death and resurrection of Jesus, uniting us in heart and soul, so that we sacrifice to meet each other's needs and seek the good of the city and live holy lives of reverent fear.

Strange and Surprising Triumph

We've seen the characters in the early chapters of Acts: the apostles in their boldness, the church in its generosity, the crowds in their need, and the Jewish leaders in their escalating hostility. We've seen the conflict: repeated collisions rooted in theological annoyance, jealousy at growth, and hatred at apostolic endurance. But what about the triumph? If good stories end well, then what do we make of the story of the early church in Jerusalem? Doesn't it end with the stoning of Stephen (7:54–60)? And doesn't this execution catalyze a widespread persecution against the whole church in Jerusalem, led by a zealous, church-ravaging Pharisee named Saul (8:1–3)?

This is perhaps the greatest lesson of this story. Yes, the stoning of Stephen and the persecution of the Jerusalem church is the end of one chapter. But it's also the beginning of another, one that shows the strange and surprising triumph of the gospel. We see the strangeness in Acts 8:4: "Now those who were scattered went about preaching the word." Not grumbling about injustice. Not blaming Stephen for bringing persecution down around them. Not despairing at Saul's harassment. They went about *preaching*. These people are exiles, refugees, outcasts from their home. But they don't act like refugees; they act like missionaries. They don't act like they got *kicked* out; they act like they got *sent* out.

The martyrdom of Stephen launches the Samaritan mission, the same mission that Jesus promised in Acts 1:8.

> "You will receive power when the Holy Spirit has come upon you, and you will be my witnesses in Jerusalem and *in all Judea and Samaria*, and to the end of the earth."

> "Now they were all scattered throughout *the regions of Judea and Samaria*." (8:1)

> "Philip went down to *the city of Samaria* and proclaimed to them the Christ." (8:5)

The Christian outcasts from Jerusalem preach to the lost outcasts of Samaria, and the Samaritans receive the good news of the kingdom of God, are baptized into the name of Jesus, and receive the Holy Spirit at apostolic hands (8:12–17). What looked like a failure was actually a prelude to success. What looked like a setback was really a setup. God had surprising purposes and plans for the good of his people and the salvation of the Samaritans and the conversion of Saul and the movement of the gospel to the ends of the earth.

This is God's way, and this is the lesson of the early chapters of Acts. Powerful preaching of the good news gathers in the refugees from the world, lost and broken by the Fall. These refugees are formed by the Spirit into a holy and resilient community that meets needs and sacrifices for others. But this same preaching threatens the rulers and authorities of this age, and they respond with opposition. Boldness in the face of such opposition escalates the hostility and violence, sometimes even leading to persecution and death. But, as Tertullian said, the blood of the martyrs is the seed of the church, and this seed always bears fruit. This is the story that God loves to tell over and over again. From Genesis to Revelation, from the early church to the present moment, God has been striking the same note in different ways in millions of stories, big and small. That note, that story, as Chesterton reminded us, is simple. Christianity, he said, has died many times. But it has always risen again, for it has a God who knows the way out of the grave.

This is the story that must mark us. This is the story that must shape our imagination and expectations in a world full of suffering and trial and persecution. From it, we learn the lesson (and may God grant us to know it deep down in our bones) that in God's world, faithful death always—*always*—leads to resurrection.

You received the word in much affliction,
with the joy of the Holy Spirit.
—1 Thessalonians 1:6

4

SUFFERING IS OUR STORY
Walking the Well-worn Path of Pain

Dieudonné Tamfu

"Turn to me and be gracious to me, for I am lonely and afflicted" (Ps. 25:16) is David's cry to God when he is surrounded by enemies. In these battles, his suffering brings acute loneliness. David feels that God has detached himself from him and from his afflictions (Ps. 10:1; 22:1; 25:16). At times, he even feels separated from the rest of humanity. "I am a worm and not a man, scorned by mankind and despised by the people" (Ps. 22:6).

Suffering tends to produce loneliness. We feel lonely, isolated, sealed off, and detached from others. It is common for us to believe that no one understands our pain. We can be deceived to think that God is distant and uncaring. While I do not wish to invalidate these emotions, I do want to extinguish the lie that the sufferer is ever alone. We are never alone in suffering because in it we join other saints in the pattern of righteous suffering that has been going on from the inception of salvation history.

Are you or other believers around you facing rejection for your faith? Do you feel lonely in your suffering? Does it seem that God is distant and has detached himself from your pain? Do you feel disappointment, bewilderment, or dismay? Are you sitting in darkness, searching for answers and grasping for hope? My hope in this chapter is to equip you to strengthen others and encourage your own soul, as you suffer for the sake of righteousness, with the following truth: *God has destined us for suffering, which has marked God's people throughout redemptive history; suffering is our story that prepares us for glory.*

Destined for Suffering

Paul addresses 1 Thessalonians to believers who are suffering for their faith in Jesus. According to the Book of Acts, after their conversion the Thessalonians were at once met with suffering. The unbelieving Jews leveled false charges against them (Acts 17:7) and incited the entire city against them (Acts 17:8). Although these believers had turned from idols to the living God (1 Thess. 1:9), become models for other churches (1:7–8), and set their hope on the return of Christ (1:10), still their repentance and good works did not insulate them from suffering. Rather they became the grounds for their suffering.

Paul writes to encourage these believers. He opens the letter with thanksgiving to God for their election, which has proven itself by the power of the gospel in their lives and the suffering they are enduring for the gospel, mirroring that of the apostles and Jesus Christ before them.

> We know, brothers loved by God, that he has chosen you, because our gospel came to you not only in word, but also in power and in the Holy Spirit and with full conviction. You know what kind of men we proved to be among you for your sake. And you became imitators of us and of the

> Lord, for you received the word in much afflic-
> tion, with the joy of the Holy Spirit. (1 Thess.
> 1:4–6)

The fact that the Thessalonians were embracing the gospel in adversity with joy affirmed to Paul that their faith was genuine.

Although Paul is glad that these afflictions have proven that the Thessalonians have set their hope on the return of Christ, he seeks to comfort them. This is where we find a model of encouragement for ourselves and others.

When their reputation is being destroyed and the whole city is up in arms against them, Paul gives the Thessalonians what their minds and hearts need: insight into God's sovereign design for all of salvation history. Paul has told them before that they would suffer. He writes, "You yourselves know that we are destined for this. For when we were with you, we kept telling you beforehand that we were to suffer affliction, just as it has come to pass, and just as you know" (1 Thess. 3:3–4). Now, in order to comfort the Thessalonians during the suffering he foretold, Paul reveals to them the pattern of suffering that they are now a part of, and the divine wisdom behind it, because Paul knows that if they better understand salvation history and God's purposes in it, then they will not be surprised by any suffering they endure for their faith.

The Pattern of Christian Suffering

First Thessalonians 2:13–16 establishes a pattern of suffering that spans through redemptive history beginning with the prophets, Jesus, the apostles, the Judean church, and now the church in Thessalonica.

> We also thank God constantly for this, that when you received the word of God, which you heard from us, you accepted it not as the word of men but as what it really is, the word of God, which is at work in you believers. For you, brothers, became imitators of the churches of God in Christ Jesus that are in Judea. For you suffered the same things from your own countrymen as they did from the Jews, who killed both the Lord Jesus and the prophets, and drove us out, and displease God and oppose all mankind by hindering us from speaking to the Gentiles that they might be saved—so as always to fill up the measure of their sins. But wrath has come upon them at last! (1 Thess. 2:13–16)

"The prophets" summarizes all those who suffered for their faith in the Old Testament (see, for instance, Matt. 5:11–12; 2 Chron. 36:16). The suffering of the righteous at the hands of the wicked is not new in redemptive history. It is an honored tradition that traverses through all of redemptive history.

After the fall of Adam in the garden of Eden, God gives the first promise of salvation, mingled with a promise of suffering: "I will put enmity between you and the woman, and between your offspring and her offspring; he shall bruise your head, and you shall bruise his heel" (Gen. 3:15). God's people would suffer in the battle between the two seeds—the seed of the woman and the seed of the serpent—and ultimate victory over the serpent would only come through suffering.

The enmity between the serpent and the seed of the woman (the unrighteous and the righteous) is first actualized after Eve gives birth to two sons. Abel is killed by Cain (Gen. 4:8) "who was of the evil one and murdered his brother" (1 John 3:12). Abel, a righteous man approved by God, is the first victim of the enemy's hatred, murdered by the first seed of the serpent.

Job suffers the loss of his health, wealth, and children when the devil himself attacks him because of his righteousness among men (Job 1:1–2:6). Joseph suffers false accusations from Potiphar's wife (Gen. 39:14–18) and imprisonment as an innocent man. Israel, God's chosen people, is afflicted and enslaved for 430 years in Egypt (Ex. 12:40), a nation led by Pharaoh, who is explicitly identified with the serpent when God calls him "the great dragon" (Ezek. 29:3; 32:2). David, God's anointed one, is hunted for several years by Saul who was rejected by God (1 Sam. 17–29). Jeremiah the prophet is persecuted by his own people after Israel has turned away from God. King Zedekiah put Jeremiah in prison for his faithfulness to God (Jer. 37). Many other prophets like Zechariah (Matt. 23:35) were killed for their faith. Jesus, the righteous Servant of God in Isaiah (Isa. 53:9), suffers because of the false accusations of the scribes and the Pharisees, who are portrayed as the offspring of the serpent (Matt. 3:7; 12:34; 23:33; Luke 3:7).[11]

11. In the Synoptic Gospels, the devil is the one who tempts Jesus (Matt. 4:1, 3; Mark 1:13; Luke 4:2) and the only other enemies that also do this are the Scribes, the Sadducees, and the Pharisees, who are the only other subjects of the verb "tempt" in the Synoptics (Matt. 16:1; 19:3; 22:18, 35; Mark 8:11; 10:2; 12:15; Luke 11:16). It is as

Christ suffers rejection, mockery, and a shameful death on a cross. This is the pinnacle of suffering among God's people, as Christ is the most righteous of them all, being sinless and without blame.

All of the righteous sufferers of the Old Testament from Abel to Zechariah pointed to Jesus, and Jesus's suffering has become the pattern for his disciples. Peter writes, "To this you have been called, because Christ also suffered for you, leaving you an example, so that you might follow in his steps" (1 Pet. 2:21).

The apostles endure much pain for their faith (Acts 5:41; 9:16). While defending his apostolic ministry, Paul gives this precise description of his suffering:

> Five times I received at the hands of the Jews the forty lashes less one. Three times I was beaten with rods. Once I was stoned. Three times I was shipwrecked; a night and a day I was adrift at sea; on frequent journeys, in danger from rivers, danger from robbers, danger from my own people, danger from Gentiles, danger in the city, danger in the wilderness, danger at sea, danger from false brothers; in toil and hardship, through many a sleepless night, in hunger and thirst, often without food, in cold and exposure. And, apart from other things, there is the daily pressure on me of my anxiety for all the churches. (2 Cor. 11:24–28)

---

though the Synoptic Gospel writers intend to show that these sects represent their father, the devil.

The churches that the apostles planted through suffering live out the same pattern (Acts 14:22; Rom. 5:3; Gal. 2:4). All kinds of saints ever since have suffered shame, mockery, and even death for their faith. There is not enough space in this book to speak of all of the Stephens and Polycarps, the Cyprians, Husses, Tyndales, and Elliots. Their precise number is only known to God (cf. Rev. 6:9–11).

When Paul tells the Thessalonians that they have become "imitators" who are "suffering the same things" that others have suffered (1 Thess. 2:14), he means that they continue the pattern of suffering from history. Using history itself as his slate, God is writing an amazing story of salvation. The protagonists are God's righteous sufferers who are being killed all the day long. Suffering is the theme and the plot. Suffering is our story.

There is a purpose for all of this suffering. In so many epic stories, as in *The Lord of the Rings*, the suffering of the protagonists leads to their glory, the triumph of good over evil, and peace for mankind. These great literary epics faintly mirror the plotline of God's redemptive work in history. The Thessalonians experience suffering, but look what results from it. They become an example to other believers (1 Thess. 1:7), their faith spreads (1:8). They will receive glory when they are found blameless at Christ's return and are caught up together with him in the air to live with him forever (4:17; 5:10). Suffering shows their election (1:4–6) and prepares them for their glorification. They can be certain that they will be blameless at the coming of Christ because God, through the fiery trials, will sanctify and keep them blameless (5:23–24).

To the contrary, the antagonists, the wicked, who afflict God's people, are filling up the measure of their sins, so wrath will finally be poured out on them (1 Thess. 2:16). God will repay with affliction those who afflict his people (2 Thess. 1:6, 8–9), while the protagonists enjoy life-giving, eternally satisfying, and restorative fellowship with their Lord, Jesus Christ (1:7).

From Righteous Abel to Righteous Yakubu

John Yakubu, a believer in Christ, is one of many contemporary righteous sufferers, treading the bloodstained, death-defying, God-honoring path of the faithful who have gone before him. *The Voice of the Martyrs* recently reported on the persecution of this righteous Nigerian believer.

John Yakubu was tortured by the Islamic group Boko Haram, and as a result, he and his family sought refuge in Cameroon. After he could no longer feed his family, he returned to his village in Nigeria to sell some of his animals. Upon reaching his village, Boko Haram militants captured him and demanded that he recant his faith in Christ and convert to Islam or suffer the consequences. Brother John denied the offer to deny his Master who had saved him. As a result, the terrorists tied him to a tree and cut both his hands with large knives. After cutting his hands, they again demanded that he convert. John replied that he would not because the terrorists could only kill the body, echoing the words of Jesus in Matthew 10:28: "Do not fear those who kill the body but cannot kill the soul. Rather fear him who can destroy both soul and body in hell." In anger the terrorists cut him on his head, back, and legs and left him to bleed to death.

In God's kindness, John was rescued and received careful medical attention. When interviewed by *Voice of the Martyrs*, he said, "I have forgiven the Islamic militants because they did not know what they were doing."[12] Through his word in Matthew 10:28, God gave John strength to endure suffering. Particularly, John received grace to endure torture through his knowledge that Christ's disciples must suffer. He remembered Christ's warning to his disciples that others would persecute them and that they should not fear. John knew that suffering would come, and he understood his role in the greater story that encompassed his life.

The Pattern Continues

You yourself may be suffering for the name of Jesus. Where do you find the encouragement to endure? Where do you find consolation in the loneliness of your grief? Look to the story of redemption, and remember that the same kinds of suffering you are experiencing are being endured by your brotherhood around the world (1 Thess. 2:14; 1 Peter 5:9). You are not alone. The story of suffering did not begin with you and will not end with you.

If you are not suffering for your faith, expect it to come. When your time comes, remember you are treading where others have trodden. That same narrow path of suffering that you tread has the bloodstained footprints of your Savior, followed by every Christian who has gone outside the city to bear the same reproach that he bore. The same grace that has sustained God's people through-

12. John Yakubu, "Nigeria: You Can't Kill My Soul," August 25, 2014. Accessed online at http://www.persecution.com/public/newsroom. aspx?story_ID=%3D373033.

out redemptive history will sustain you, if you trust him. The grace that empowered Peter and the apostles to proclaim, "We must obey God rather than men" (Acts 5:29), the same grace that enabled Stephen to pray for forgiveness as rocks were hurled at his broken body (Acts 7:59–60), the same grace that empowered Ignatius of Antioch to say, "Come fire and cross and grapplings with wild beasts, the rending of my bones and body . . . only let it be mine to attain Jesus Christ,"[13] the same grace that emboldened Polycarp to declare, "86 years have I have served him, and he has done me no wrong—how can I blaspheme my King and my Savior?," the same grace that empowered Luther to say, "Here I stand"—this is the same grace that will empower you to suffer well as you pursue righteousness in Christ, guarding the truth, and calling what is evil "evil" and what is good "good."

The same glory that they have received is awaiting you. At the end of this path of suffering stained with the blood, tears, and pain of the saints lies a glorious inheritance that will make the longest trial on earth seem very ephemeral. All who suffer for Christ await an eternity of no tears, no pain, and an everlasting inheritance, chief of which is our scar-handed Savior who will be our everlasting and all-satisfying delight.

If you endure your suffering with joy, like the Thessalonians, the saints of old, and John Yakubu, you will be an example for others, your faith and the gospel of Jesus Christ will be greatly prized through you, and God will be greatly glorified in your life, as he sanctifies and guards

---

13. John Foxe and the Voice of the Martyrs, *Foxe: Voices of the Martyrs,* (Bartlesville, OK: VOM Books, 2007), 52.

your faith through the fires of the established pattern of excruciating suffering. To that end, I pray with Paul for you, "that our God may make you worthy of his calling and may fulfill every resolve for good and every work of faith by his power, so that the name of our Lord Jesus may be glorified in you, and you in him, according to the grace of our God and the Lord Jesus Christ" (2 Thess. 1:11–12).

The sufferings of this present time are not worth comparing with the glory that is to be revealed to us.
–Romans 8:18

5

NOT WORTH COMPARING

Faith and Hope in the Face of Persecution

Steve Timmis

I sit writing this in the aftermath of a terrorist attack on Paris, a city that is a mere four-hour train ride from my home. More than 350 people were injured; 130 killed brutally, senselessly. The city of Brussels, a similar distance away, is under virtual lockdown. Passenger planes have been bombed out of the sky in recent months. A fighter jet obliterated by a missile. The world seems a more dangerous place now than it did even a mere year ago. At the same time, my own government is considering fighting extremism by requiring all religious ministers to undergo screening and some form of registration.

How should I respond to these threats, real or apparent? The future seems more uncertain and life more tenuous. My natural instinct is to be fearful and apprehensive, but the Spirit of God within me will not let those emotions dictate. My conscience is troubled, and my affections stirred for *something better*.

Peter was writing to groups of Christians scattered around the area we now know as Turkey. Evidently, they were isolated, marginalized, despised, and harassed. It is shocking to many of us to see how apparently insensitive Peter was to their plight. At no point does he empathize with them, or even offer them much sympathy. He simply talks about the *something better* in terms of the testing of their faith, the presence of the Spirit, and the inexpressible joy that is already tinged with glory itself.

But how do we move from fear to faith?

The Joseph Plan

One of the lessons I learned early in ministry was what I call "the Joseph Plan." The Joseph Plan is delightfully simple and profoundly helpful. You may remember the narrative in Genesis 41. Joseph was tasked with interpreting Pharaoh's dream. It turns out that there were seven years of famine ahead, but they would be preceded by seven years of plenty. Pharaoh needed to appoint someone who could oversee the project to store up in the years of plenty enough food to sustain the country during the years of unprecedented famine. Joseph was the right man in the right place at the right time—providence!

The Joseph Plan is a helpful model for how we prepare the people of God for suffering. The best time to teach people about the sovereignty of God is in those times when the truth is not under threat from adverse circumstances. We need to learn to celebrate the precious doctrine of divine inscrutability, even as Paul does: "How unsearchable are his judgments and how inscrutable his ways!" (Rom. 11:33). We simply do not know why God does what he does in the way that he does it. But that is not the end of the story, because although his ways are inscrutable, his character is not. We know that he is always, only, and truly good. We know that because of the cross of his dear Son and our beautiful Savior. But the Joseph Plan helps us see that the people of God need this teaching from the Scriptures when life is not a "riddle wrapped in a mystery inside an enigma."[14] We pastors and teachers in the church need to help our people store up the riches of gospel truth in the times of abundance and ease, so that when suffering comes, they will not want.

Such a perspective cannot be assumed. So many of us, in the Western world at least, have lived under the misapprehension that suffering is an anomaly. We fondly imagined that the years of plenty will not end, and that difficulties and trials will not come. Persecution is endured by other people in other places and at other times, but it is not something to trouble us much.

Peter's telling exhortation shows us that it is otherwise. "Fiery trials" (1 Pet. 4:12) are not strange, and so it turns out, neither should they be thought of as the famine years. Peter assumes all the way through his epistle that suffering for Christ is, in fact, the banquet of the soul.

You may read that with a certain incredulity. But that is probably because, like me, you are someone who has known relatively little suffering for Christ. Of course, I have suffered some. I have endured trials. I have passed through personal difficulties and heartaches. But overt persecution on account of being a Christian has been strangely absent from my life. Some of that is due, I am sure, to my hesitancy to speak of Christ when opportunity presented itself. Though most of it I think is because of the peculiar historical circumstances of living in a society still ignorantly feeding off the vestiges of a Judeo-Christian heritage.

14. Winston Churchill, *BBC Broadcast*, London, October 1, 1939.

That is not the case for many people in the world, just as it was not the case for our brothers and sisters who lived throughout the totalitarian regime that once covered around fifteen percent of the earth's land mass, known as the Soviet Union.

I traveled from time to time into the so-called "evil empire"[15] towards the tail end of its life. I visited people and churches who were part of the Unregistered Baptists. It was all very discreet and clandestine. Addresses had to be memorized. Buses hopped. Authorities avoided. Strangers treated with suspicion. I once had the rather surreal experience of meeting with two of the main leaders of the denomination who had been "underground" for over twenty years. They were wanted by the authorities, with a price on their heads, but here was I, eating borsch with them in a small apartment, a stone throw away from the notorious KGB headquarters!

On a later occasion, I arrived at a church meeting in a rough cabin, at the edge of a forest in the heart of a bitter winter. It was early in the morning and bitingly cold at negative 35 degrees Celsius. It happened to be the final day of a meeting of church leaders from around the region. As I walked up the path, one of the men I had shared a bowl of borsch with saw me and greeted me warmly. This put the others at ease, and I had the privilege of filing through a guard of fifty pastors who, following the example of their leader, all kissed me on the lips. This was the conventional greeting between men in this Baptist sub-culture. It was not my place to critique their practices or rebut their

15. Ronald Reagan, "Remarks at the Annual Convention of the National Association of Evangelicals in Orlando, Florida," March 8, 1983.

welcome. My lips were sore and chapped by the end of the procession, but what an immense privilege to be so honored by lips that had refused to kiss Stalin's ring.

It was an even greater privilege to spend time with these pastors. These were men who knew what it was to suffer for Christ, and they knew how to suffer well. I cannot recall a single conversation characterized by self-pity or regret. If I was talking to a pastor who had spent over thirty years in a camp in Siberia, he rejoiced that he had been counted worthy to suffer for his Lord. If I spoke with a woman who had been deprived of her husband for twelve of the fifteen years they had been married, she was thankful for the sufficiency of God's grace. If I spoke with children who had endured ridicule and punishment in the school system because of their refusal to disown their Savior, they were encouraged that Jesus knew of their pain.

I went into the meeting and sat through a three-hour service of singing, weeping, praying, and preaching. There were typically three sermons in each meeting, and almost always the theme of each one was the return of Christ—as it was for many of the haunting hymns we sang together.

These were people who had a grasp on eternity that was almost entirely alien to me. My exposure to the Second Coming came in the forms of either asinine millennial discussions or graphic cartoons about the secret rapture. But these were men and women who cherished the thought of Christ's return and nourished their souls on the delectable promise of glory.

On the early trips, I would breathe a sigh of relief as our plane left the runway at Sheremetyevo International Airport, north of Moscow. Relieved to be heading home. Relieved to escape the suffocating atmosphere of oppression with its ubiquitous sense of menace. But as I was exposed to more and more stories, and witnessed first-hand more and more examples of simple but daring gospel faithfulness, I noticed my perspective changing. I was always glad to be leaving Moscow, but I now did so without a smug, self-satisfied sense of pity. Or maybe it was even replaced with an appropriate sense of self-pity? Those of us in the "free" West were the ones needing sympathy. We were the ones seduced by "the good life" so that life was defined by what we had this side of the grave. Any thought of eternity was dismissed out of hand as "pie in the sky when you die," or corrected by talk of "steak on the plate while you wait." Of course, many of us would never espouse prosperity theology in a formal sense, but functionally it was the framework within which many of us often operated.

We still do. The analogy of the rich getting into heaven being harder than a camel passing through the eye of a needle is unsettling only for those of us who are rich— those seduced by the accouterments of wealth. State-sponsored persecution has not been our daily experience, but Satan has had his own strategy to distract us—and a very effective strategy it has proved to be. Just as a child's hunger can be satiated with marshmallows, so too our hungry souls can be easily fooled into thinking they are full with fancies and morsels. So we trade the real for the imitation, the milk for the froth, the cake for the crumbs. But the word of God tells us that there is a more desirable exchange. Faithfulness to Christ may mean we lose all that this world has to give, and even our very lives, but as Jesus himself asked, "What does it profit a man to gain the whole world and forfeit his soul?" (Mark 8:36).

I love that verse in Revelation 12:11 where John writes about the accuser of the brethren being thrown down because "they have conquered him by the blood of the Lamb and by the word of their testimony, for they loved not their lives even unto death." It is my prayer, and increasingly so, that I might not merely live well, but that I might also die well to the glory of God and for the fame of the Savior. That may be in the comfort of my own bed. It may yet be in a prison cell, or by an angry mob or at the hands of isis. But whatever the future holds, we should nourish our souls on the bread of heaven, so that we might feast with him in glory.

At the end of that church service I mentioned above, I was invited to bring a final word. As I was just outside Leningrad, I took the opportunity of telling the church about the privilege I had as a teenager of wearing a bracelet bearing the name of a prisoner to prompt me to pray. The prisoner in question was Aida Skripnokova.[16] I spoke about how I had prayed for her regularly, read her story often, and was deeply challenged by her fortitude in the face of suffering. There was an audible response from many in the congregation.

At the end of the service, I was standing next to the log fire, warming myself before heading out into the icy cold. A group of *babushkas* came toward me with tears in their eyes. They stood in front of me, talking excitedly, and then introduced me to Aida herself. It was an unforgettable moment. Speaking with this small, gracious woman who had defied the might of the Soviet State because of

16. Aida's story is told by Michael Bordeaux in *Aida of Leningrad*, rev. ed. (Mowbray: 1976).

her fidelity to Christ was truly humbling. She didn't think there was anything strange about the fiery trial she had endured. Rather, she rejoiced because she shared in the sufferings of Christ, because she knew she would rejoice all the more when his glory is revealed. As she said, echoing Paul from Romans 8:18, "My suffering? It is not worth comparing."

Maranatha! Come, Lord Jesus!

Those who look to him are radiant,
and their faces shall never be ashamed.
–Psalm 34:5

6

RADIANT AND UNASHAMED

Resurrection Light in the Growing Darkness

Tim Keesee

Day after day, report after sickening report from the Middle East and Africa seep like puncture wounds. They describe the suffering of Christians—beatings, kidnappings, enslavement, as well as rape, beheading, even crucifixion. It's twenty-first-century persecution with first-century methods of murder. Both the scale of the suffering, as well as the gap between us and it, is enormous. Our ability to identify with suffering believers will likely grow over time, as the cold waves of intimidation creep up to our schools, offices, and church doors—and it's not high tide yet. But for now, on our side, reports of Christian persecution are too often met with a quick prayer, a sentimental cliché, a shrugging indifference, or eye-averting embarrassment; but the blood is red, the bruises black, and the injustice unanswerable.

A few years ago while in Pakistan, I tracked down a pastor who had been beaten nearly to death by a Muslim mob, while the police stood by and watched. The pastor's offense? He had the nerve to try to protect women in his church from assault. I wrote in my journal that night,

In the hospital ward, forty men were housed
with Pastor Indriaz. Cats darted in and out of
the room, and flies lingered over the blood-spat-
tered floor. The left side of the young pastor's
head was smashed in. The beating severed his ear
and left him blind in one eye. Because of convul-
sions, his wrists were awkwardly tied with cords
to the sides of his bed, leaving him in a position
of twisted agony. His wife, Shinaz, sat next to
him, holding their three-month-old son. She
stared blankly at her husband with indescribable
sadness in her eyes, as the baby nuzzled her and
cried softly.

It seems clear that the doctors had hoped
Indriaz would be dead by now, and they are
uncomfortable with the attention his case is now
getting. Before I left, Indriaz began to stir and
fixed his one eye on me. Who can describe the
sorrow in that eye—or the anger I feel tonight?

I'm still angry. I'm angry over my brothers' and sisters' sufferings and frustrated over our inability to make much of a
difference, even with great effort. Even when we can help
a few brothers and sisters in their need, there are hundreds
more we can't get to—and thousands more we haven't even
heard about.

But can't the government do something? As someone
who has worked on and off Capitol Hill for years, advoca-
cy efforts to leverage government intervention are limited
and often discouraging. There are a few Josephs and Dan-
iels there who labor on behalf of their suffering brothers
and sisters. But overall, the amount of effort expended to

get people in power to use their power to speak and act on behalf of persecuted Christians is enormous—it seems at times we would get a better hearing if we simply stood on a street corner and shouted.

And the official deafness to the killing of Christians isn't just in America. Lord David Alton sounded like a voice crying in the wilderness when on the floor of the British Parliament he challenged his government's indifference to the plight of Christians in Syria, whose population since 2003—either by the coffin or the suitcase—has dropped from 1.5 million to less than 200,000 today. Alton said, "This is a genocide that dares not speak its name . . . either there is a genocide underway or there is not; either there is worldwide persecution of Christians or there is not; either someone is being killed, imprisoned or tortured every few minutes for reasons of faith or belief, or they are not."[17]

To the Hard Places

This bleak picture isn't a call for inaction or for more passive pieties. We have all of that in abundance already. Christians are called to go to the hard places. They are called not to save their lives but to spend them for Christ. They are called to proclaim the gospel and to adorn that message through lives of compassion and sacrifice. These observations are only to underscore the reality of our limitations—our suffering brothers and sisters are weak and vulnerable to the next evil man with a gun or grenade,

17. Lord David Alton, from House of Lords debate on Universal Declaration on Human Rights: Article 18, Thursday, October 22, 2015, London, England.

and we are weak (even with our best efforts) to help them and vulnerable to pressures closer to home. Though we are in different settings and dangers, yet we are all like lambs—easily kicked, easily beaten, easily killed. Like jars of clay, we are so easily broken, but that is "to show that the surpassing power belongs to God and not to us. We are afflicted in every way, but not crushed; perplexed, but not driven to despair; persecuted, but not forsaken; struck down, but not destroyed; always carrying in the body the death of Jesus, so that the life of Jesus may also be manifested in our bodies" (2 Cor. 4:7–10).

In the midst of every kind of sorrow and suffering, the Risen King keeps the last promise he made to us: "I am with you always." Always. By the time Christ made this promise, he had forever crushed the power of death; so his promise is good on both sides of the grave. "Neither death nor life . . . will be able to separate us from the love of God in Christ Jesus our Lord" (Rom. 8:38–39).

This is why "those who look to him are radiant, and their faces shall never be ashamed" (Ps. 34:5). Their faces are radiant because they reflect the presence of the risen Christ. Perhaps this explains Stephen's appearance as he preached the gospel for the last time. "Gazing at him, all who sat in the council saw that his face was like the face of an angel" (Acts 6:15). Stephen could give radiant witness to the gospel because he was living out the unshakeable reality of his unending life in Christ.

Jesus Is Real

Radiant, unashamed witness is still shaking the gates of hell. In North Africa, Sayid spent his first thirty years in the utter darkness of Islam. He was drawn to the light through listening to Christian broadcasts and eventually believed on Jesus. Christ lit the candle of Sayid's life, and he couldn't conceal it. "A city set on a hill cannot be hidden" (Matt. 5:14). The day Sayid was baptized, he sent a group message to over one hundred people—everyone in his phone contact list. It said simply, "Walit Masihi." "I have become a Christian." In his 99.9% Muslim country, this was like asking to be killed. But Sayid did not have a death wish—he has a living hope. In fact, his old life was the real death sentence. But not now. Now in Christ he has never been more alive—a life that no man can ever take away.

Though Sayid has been arrested and beaten and has had many death threats over the years, this disciple is himself a disciple-maker and pastor. I gathered with his little congregation for worship and heard testimonies of transforming grace. One brother named Kamal said his first exposure to the gospel was through Christian satellite TV. The one thing that stood out to him was that, whereas a Muslim's standard prayer was for Allah to kill all non-Muslims, he heard Christians praying for all peoples. Kamal saw a way of love and grace that led straight to Christ. He told me the word "salvation" occurs nowhere in the Koran, but the Bible is all about salvation. So Kamal believed on Jesus, the Messiah, and prayed to him at the only place he knew to pray: the mosque.

He had never met another Christian. But one day at the café where he was a waiter, he greeted a man with the salutation, "Peace and grace." The standard Arabic greeting is usually, "Salam" (peace). Kamal said, "Peace *and grace*." The man he said it to, whose name was Mohammed and who also was a believer, said, "Are you a Christian?" Kamal said he was, saying he prayed to Christ in the mosque. Mohammed said, "No. You don't need to go to the mosque to pray. You can pray anywhere. Anytime. Christ is in you. And you don't need to clean yourself by the ceremonial washing because Christ has forever washed you by his blood." Later, these two newfound brothers baptized each other in the sea near their city.

The truth Mohammed taught Kamal—Christ is in you—flows from Kamal with all its life, joy, and witness. As a result, he twice lost his job, and he and his family have been evicted from their apartment. But this truth has also flowed in life-giving witness to others at the house church meeting. Kamal's brother-in-law, Hasan, told me that when the September 11, 2001 attack occurred in the United States and thousands of innocent people were murdered in the name of Islam, he rejected Islam in his heart. So when Kamal shared Christ with him, he immediately believed the gospel.

Another brother named Haroun said that in times of betrayal and police raids, whenever he is in the grip of fear, his response is to pray—and then to immediately go out and tell someone about Jesus. In the name of Jesus, demons are cast out—and in the name of Jesus fear is cast out, too.

For Sayid, Kamal, Mohammed, Hasan, and Haroun, speaking the gospel in the face of real risks is driven by the reality that Jesus is not just a charming name, nor is he a bit of wishful thinking. He is a living Person, and he is really with them. It's the power of his resurrection on display through them.

Risen and Radiant

Near the end of his extraordinary ministry, Samuel Zwemer, pioneer missionary to Arabia, preached the following.

> It is time that a protest be made against the misuse of the word "evangelism." It has only one etymological, New Testament, historical, and theological connotation; namely, to tell the good news of One who came to earth to die on the cross for us: who rose again and who ever lives to intercede with those who repent and believe the Gospel. To evangelize is to win disciples, to become fishers of men, to carry the Gospel message directly to all the nations. Even prayer, private and public, is not evangelism and should not be its substitute. We may pray for our friends and relatives. But do we ever evangelize them? It is so much easier to talk about them to Christ than to talk to them about Christ. Even our lives cannot bear full witness to Christ without our lips. If we are ashamed of the Gospel message our lives will not be radiant.[18]

Radiant. There must have been something of that about Peter and John as they stood before the council and declared that salvation is in Jesus alone. Who were these men to speak such things to the supreme court of the land? They were without credentials or degrees. But there was something about Peter and John, something about their

---

18. Samuel Zwemer, from the message "The Cross in Christ's Commission," preached at Urbana 1946 in Toronto, Canada.

courage, something about the stand-alone force of their words, something—no, *someone*.

Did the faces of Caiaphas and his cronies suddenly turn pale? "Didn't we get rid of him? Crucified, buried, gone for good?" The person who wouldn't go away was now reflected in the faces and words of his disciples, and there was no denying it. "They recognized that they had been with Jesus" (Acts 4:13).

In this darkening hour, we are weak and vulnerable, but Christ is a champion without rival. So look up! The veil is torn. See our radiant, risen King who will never abandon any of his people. Through the power of his unending life and unbroken grace, he is in us and with us and for us. Always.

Blessed be the God and Father of our Lord Jesus Christ,
the Father of mercies and God of all comfort,
who comforts us in all our affliction,
so that we may be able to comfort those who are in any affliction,
with the comfort with which we ourselves are comforted by God.
—2 Corinthians 1:3–4

7

THE FELLOWSHIP OF THE SUFFERING

Rejoicing Together in Fiery Trials

D. Glenn

Several years ago, our first child was born prematurely. He died shortly after he was born. It was one of the most difficult times of our lives. In the beginning, we felt so alone. As time went on, though, we came to know a number of families who also have lost infants. We seem to simply find each other. Friends or co-workers introduce us. We are from different places, and each of us has a different story, yet we immediately have a deep connection as we open up and share about our loss. There is mutual comfort and encouragement in this particular fellowship of the suffering.

We found that when we talked with others who had experienced similar pain, there was no need to explain ourselves. Even when we expressed anger or fears or other emotions that many seek to avoid, there was no need to avoid them with these fellow sufferers because they had all felt it too.

This fellowship of the suffering is not only among those who have suffered in the same ways we had. I specifically remember one friend. She has suffered terribly from cluster headaches and migraines. At times they have been debilitating. As we sat with her shortly after our son had died, we received real comfort and grace through her.

I later realized that even though she had not suffered exactly like us, she had still suffered in a way that had changed her. Her suffering was so deep and significant that her life had been altered. She still held onto her faith in God, but she did not view the world in the same way she had before. She had lost her innocence, just like we had. She had come to the end of herself in the midst of the suffering and found that God is still a sure foundation.

So one way the fellowship of the suffering brings comfort is by all the members of the fellowship passing on the comfort they have received. God comforts us so that we, in turn, can comfort others "with the comfort with which we ourselves are comforted by God" (2 Cor. 1:4). There is another way this fellowship comforts as well. Comfort comes in the mere knowledge that I am not the only one who has suffered. Indeed, suffering is the norm, and therefore what I am experiencing is not unique.

The Normalcy of the Fellowship

One of the hardest and most difficult things about living in the West is that our lives have become so easy and comfortable. We have come to expect comfort and ease, even believing at times that it is our right. Suffering seems to be an anomaly in our lives, not the norm. It certainly is not the expectation. However, for the apostle Peter, suffering is not merely acknowledged; it is assumed. He knows that his readers "have been grieved by various trials" (1 Pet. 1:6). He expects that they would be slandered (2:12; 3:16) and emphasizes that the path of suffering was the one marked out by Jesus, and is the path we ought to follow him in. "Christ also suffered for you, leaving you an example, so that you might follow in his steps" (2:21).

For Peter, suffering should not be a surprise. He says in 4:12–13, "Beloved, do not be surprised at the fiery trial when it comes upon you to test you, as though something strange were happening to you. But rejoice insofar as you share Christ's sufferings, that you may also rejoice and be glad when his glory is revealed."

We will all suffer. The Bible is clear about this. Paul encouraged his disciples, telling them, "Through many tribulations we must enter the kingdom of God" (Acts 14:22). If we do have any doubts about it, we only need to look at the world around us. Poverty. Injustice. Sickness. War. Death.

Unfortunately, many of us are surprised when suffering comes because our suffering seems strange to us. We have believed that we should not suffer or, perhaps, could not suffer. It is as if we believe the blessing of God shields us from pain, rather than recognizing that often it is in the pain that we find the blessing. Peter clearly states that the fiery trial will come, and we ought not think it is something strange when it does. It should be seen as something normal.

Therefore, it should not call into question the character, purpose, goodness, or promises of God. Jesus himself told us to expect it. If the world hated him, it will hate his disciples as well. If it persecuted him, it will persecute them also (John 15:18–20). It should be no surprise, then, when we suffer, and it is no reason for us to think something strange is happening.

Peter says something similar regarding the normalcy of suffering in 1 Peter 5:8–10.

> Be sober-minded; be watchful. Your adversary the devil prowls around like a roaring lion, seeking someone to devour. Resist him, firm in your faith, knowing that the same kinds of suffering are being experienced by your brotherhood throughout the world. And after you have suffered a little while, the God of all grace, who has called you to his eternal glory in Christ, will himself restore, confirm, strengthen, and establish you.

The devil seeks to destroy. We must resist him. One thing that can help us resist him is the simple knowledge that the devil also seeks to devour others. The same kinds of suffering I experience are shared by brothers and sisters throughout the world as well.

The main command is to resist the devil, but key to resisting is remaining firm in faith *and* knowing that others are also experiencing the same kinds of suffering. In my suffering, I am not alone. Those before me have suffered and endured. Right now others throughout the world are suffering and enduring. This simple truth ought to give me grace and strength to resist the devil and his wicked schemes.

The devil's main line of attack is to make us doubt the goodness of God. If he can convince me that I alone am suffering, I will be tempted to think that God does not love me or that I have uniquely done something to lose God's favor. I will be tempted to believe that my suffering is a sign of my rejection. However, can I believe such a thing if I know that other brothers and sisters, those loved by God, are also suffering?

An Example of the Fellowship

We live in the Middle East now and work among Syrian refugees. One of the greatest blessings in our work is that we get to work alongside other Arab believers, including some Iraqis who are themselves refugees. These are Christian-background Iraqis who had to flee their homeland due to increasing threats from Islamists, especially ISIS. Since the fall of Saddam Hussein in 2003, Islamic terrorist groups like Al Qaeda and ISIS have spread terror throughout Iraq. After the civil war started in Syria, ISIS was able to expand there as well. They are killing Muslims and Christians alike, but the Christian community in particular has been hard hit by ISIS, especially after they took over Mosul, Iraq's second largest city, in 2014. Many Christians have been forced to flee for their lives, losing all their possessions in the process. Some of those who have sought refuge still have a heart for other refugees, including Syrian Muslims who have fled their country. It is a privilege to work alongside of them.

The depth of this privilege became clear to me one day as we listened to Abu Yusef share his testimony of how God had delivered him when he had been kidnapped in Iraq. Some men took him and threw him into a trunk of a car. As they drove along, he suspected they would kill him. Terrorists would kidnap people, often Christians, and demand ransom. After it was paid, they sometimes killed them anyway.

On the road, they passed over a big bump that jarred the trunk open. Abu Yusef had a bag over his head and his hands were tied, but he knew this was his only chance. He threw himself out of the trunk and landed on a busy street with some police officers nearby. The car did not bother to stop, but just sped off and he was saved.

Hearing this firsthand was quite moving and shocking. I was encouraged as he shared about God's grace, power, and deliverance. But then, one of the other Iraqi guys simply said, "Yeah, that happened to me too." He also had been kidnapped. Later another Iraqi joined the ministry. He too had been kidnapped (as had his daughter). All three of these men had experienced fiery trials at the hands of Islamic terrorists. And yet there they were, serving Syrian Muslim refugees in the name of Jesus.

Their experiences did not lead them to fear, hatred, and bitterness. Instead, it led them to love, forgiveness, and mercy. One was asked what he would do if he saw his kidnappers. He simply responded, "I would hug them and tell them I love them and that Christ died for them."

THE POWER OF THE FELLOWSHIP

This response is possible because they belong to the fellowship of the suffering. They draw strength from one another and refuse to despair in the midst of their suffering precisely because they know they are not the first, nor will they be the last.

When they were kidnapped and faced the possibility of death if the ransom was not paid or if they refused to become Muslims, they were not surprised. It was not strange. And therefore they did not start questioning

God's goodness. The possibility of kidnapping because of their Christian faith was already real and settled in their minds. The fact that others had faced this trial, even those who had been killed, gave them strength to not forsake Jesus in the midst of it. The normalcy of this suffering among their brethren gave them power to endure. It was not a surprise, and therefore, they were not tempted to believe God had rejected them.

Was this not the encouragement that Elijah needed when he felt that he alone worshiped Yahweh? Elijah had faithfully served God and stood up to the false prophets. Yet what was the result? Jezebel sought to kill him. He was on the run, so discouraged that he even hoped he could die (1 Kings 19:4). He had been jealous for God's name, but in the end everyone had turned aside and he alone was left facing this trial (1 Kings 19:14). Except he was not alone. God was keeping seven thousand who also had not bowed the knee to Baal (1 Kings 19:18). The simple knowledge that he was not alone gave him the power to press on.

The Glory of the Fellowship

Of course, it is not only with other Christians that we share in this fellowship of the suffering. Most significantly, we share in this fellowship with Jesus Christ (Phil. 3:10). Peter not only tells us not to be surprised when the trials come, but also to rejoice in those trials. "Rejoice insofar as you share Christ's sufferings, that you may also rejoice and be glad when his glory is revealed" (1 Pet. 4:13). Rather than be shocked when we suffer, we are to celebrate. Rather than be astonished, we are to count it all joy (James 1:2). Be it in the Middle East or in North America.

We rejoice not because fiery trials are good. They are not. We rejoice because in our fiery trials we share with Christ in his. We rejoice because sharing in Christ's suffering means we also will share with him in his glory. We are, after all, "heirs of God and fellow heirs with Christ, *provided* we suffer with him in order that we may also be glorified with him" (Rom. 8:17). It is by sharing in Christ's sufferings that we share in his glory. It is when we know the pain of dying with Christ that we are able to fully experience the glory of being raised with him.

The good news in our suffering is not that God will help us endure (though he will). The good news is that after we have endured, God will glorify us with his own Son. The good news is that when his glory is revealed, we will share in that glory.

We experience real pain and real heartache here. However, we know that we are one among many of our brothers and sisters who also suffer such pain and heartache. The fiery trials are not ours alone. They are for all of Christ's body. And we are able to endure them because we do not experience them by ourselves, but as members of the fellowship of the suffering, whose head is none other than Jesus the Christ.

As members of the fellowship of the suffering we also become members in the fellowship of the glorified. Our "light momentary affliction is preparing for us an eternal weight of glory beyond all comparison" (2 Cor. 4:17). This is not an individual promise; it is a corporate promise. It is for all members of the body of Christ who follow in the footsteps of our suffering Savior on the road to Calvary, whether in Iraq or in the United States. It is for all who have died with him—whatever insults, whatever maligning, whatever kidnapping, whatever persecution—in order that we might also be raised with him to the glory that will never end.

Above all, keep loving one another earnestly,
since love covers a multitude of sins.
−1 Peter 4:8

8

WHEN OPPOSITION IS FROM WITHIN

Loving Each Other, Even as It Hurts

Tim Cain

I grew up reading missionary biographies about men and women who took great risks for God and suffered tremendously because of them. They were my heroes, and I dreamed of following in their footsteps. Of course, to do that I thought I would have to move somewhere dangerous where the gospel was strongly opposed, and people were persecuted for their faith. At that time, the only category I had for Christian suffering was external persecution.

My college professors tried to broaden my horizons. In order to prepare me for the ministry, they told me story after story of how horribly they had been treated by people in the church. They assured me that there would be no shortage of opportunities to suffer.

I don't know why I didn't pay more attention to them. Somehow I thought if you just loved other Christians and treated them with respect, they would respond by treating you the same way. Even if this wasn't true of all Christians, I was convinced that it would at least be true of the leaders in the church.

And then one day, I found myself sitting in the associate pastor's office. I had just moved across the country to help lead the youth group, and I was excited and scared about what this next stage of my life might hold. The first thing that this pastor told me was that he didn't like me, and that he completely disagreed with the church's decision to let me move out here. As I sat there, speechless, his intensity grew as he told me that he didn't trust me and threatened that if I ever did anything to jeopardize his job security or the welfare of his family, he would personally make sure that I paid for it. The snarl in his voice and the malice in his eyes left me trembling as I got up to leave his office.

I didn't know Christians could treat each other like that. I didn't think a pastor would talk like that to their worst enemies, let alone to someone who was trying their best to tell students about Jesus and his love. Basically I didn't know that fiery trials could come from inside the church as well as from the outside.

But I do now. I know that the worst pain I have ever experienced has come from people I loved and trusted in the church, and I am certain that I am not alone. A good portion of the tears that have been shed in my office have been shed by people who were hurt by other Christians. The church is supposed to be a family. We have been adopted by God the Father and called to love one another the same way that he has loved us. It's a beautiful picture that speaks to the deep longings of our heart. Yet the scars we bear from each other are a daily reminder of just how far short of this picture we have fallen.

Opposition from Within

It really shouldn't surprise us that opposition can come from inside as well as outside. It has been that way from the very beginning. Jesus came to his own people, and his own did not receive him (John 1:11). He was betrayed by one of his own disciples. Paul warns the Ephesian elders that after his departure, "Fierce wolves will come in among you, not sparing the flock; and *from among your own selves* will arise men speaking twisted things, to draw away the disciples after them" (Acts 20:29–30). One of Paul's good friends deserted him, and then when the time came for his first defense, he found that no one was willing to stand up with him (2 Tim. 4:9, 16). From the very beginning, some of the greatest trials have come from within.

So what do we do when it happens to us? How are we supposed to respond to the fiery trials that come from within? What do you do when you find out that

- someone you thought really liked you has been putting you down behind your back?
- someone you confided in about your sin decides that they no longer want to be associated with you?
- someone you poured yourself out for isn't there to help you when you have a need?
- someone you trusted as a leader turns out to be living a double life?
- someone you loved deeply as a friend and thought would always be there for you decides to leave the church in order to pursue an inappropriate relationship?

- someone you hurt chooses not to forgive you even though you tell him over and over again how sorry you are?
- someone who made you some really big promises decides not to keep them?

How will you respond to the trials that come from within? Will you leave your local church with the hopes of finding another church where things like this won't happen? Will you pull back from the church and begin seeing it more as a service to attend than a family to be a part of? Will you fall into self-pity and wonder why this is happening to you after all of the sacrifices you have made for God and his people? Will you build walls and decide that the safest way to navigate the local church is to love fewer people and to love them less?

That's the temptation, isn't it? To pull back, to build walls, to protect ourselves so that we won't get hurt like this again. We make heroes of the martyrs who risk their lives in order to love the lost, but we somehow think that the right response to the trials that come from within the church is to protect ourselves.

Why? Why do we tell our missionaries that it's good to take risks and be persecuted for loving the lost while we tell ourselves that it's good to build walls and protect ourselves from being hurt by each other?

The answer isn't that hard. No one likes to suffer. It's one thing to talk about a theology of suffering, but it's another thing completely to embrace that theology with our lives. It's easy to praise the risks of another, but it's very different to take those risks ourselves. Yet that is precisely what Peter is calling us all to do in 1 Peter 4:8 when he writes, "Above all, keep loving one another earnestly, since love covers a multitude of sins."

Peter is calling us to respond to the fiery trials that come from within the church not by pulling back from one another, but by pushing in; not by punishing people, but by sacrificing for them; not by keeping track of their sins, but by covering them; not by loving less, but by loving more. Peter comes and says above all else to keep loving each other, even when it's hard, even when you are hurt, even when you are sinned against, even when others aren't loving you the way that you are loving them. Nevertheless, "keep loving one another earnestly, since love covers a multitude of sins."

Recipe for Heartbreak

Now, those of us who have tried this know that it's a recipe for heartbreak. C. S. Lewis was right when he said, "To love at all is to be vulnerable. Love anything and your heart will certainly be wrung and possibly be broken."[19] The love that Peter is talking about comes with a cost. This earnest love, this no-matter-what love, this covers-a-multitude-of-sins love will inevitably lead to suffering.

Of course, Peter knew that as well as anyone. You see, when Peter talks about this kind of love, he isn't dreaming of some ideal; he is remembering the way that he has been loved. He is remembering the night when he failed in ways that he never imagined possible; the night where he wasn't the victim of a fiery trial, but the cause; the night where he stood around a charcoal fire and denied three times that he

19. *The Four Loves* (New York: Harcourt Brace Jovanovich, 1960), 169.

even knew who Jesus was. Peter spent the rest of that night weeping bitterly as he came to grips with the depth of his sin. Peter thought that it was over. He knew that no matter what happened next, there would be no going back after what he had done.

But Peter was wrong. Peter was wrong because what happened next was the Son of God went to the cross, and there he suffered and died so that he could keep on loving his people even after all of their rebellion. There the Lamb of God shed his precious blood to cover the multitude of our sins.

Then Jesus rose again from the dead and went out to find Peter. The risen Lord built a charcoal fire and stooped down to make his disciples breakfast. There around that fire, Jesus restored Peter and entrusted him with the work of the ministry. It was there that Peter grasped the earnestness of his Savior's love and realized that it was big enough to cover the multitude of his sins.

Let me ask you, have you experienced what Peter did? Have you been struck by the depths of your own depravity? Have you been overwhelmed by the multitude of your sins? Until you know the multitude of your sins, you will never be able to experience the love that is able to cover them all.

But if you are willing to confess your sins, you will find that Jesus is "faithful and just to forgive [your] sins and cleanse [you] from all [your] unrighteousness" (1 John 1:9). You will know then that he has never stopped loving you and that his blood is sufficient to cover all of your sins. That is what true love looks like. "By this we know love, that he laid down his life for us, and we ought to lay down our lives for the brothers" (1 John 3:16).

We have been loved with a costly love that was big enough to cover over all our sins, and now we have been called to love one another with this same love. How do we respond to the fiery trials that come from within? We love.

We love one another when it's hard. We love one another when we are hurt. We love one another when we are sinned against. We love one another even when it feels like we are the only ones doing it. We love one another this way because that is exactly how our Savior has loved us.

This love may be difficult, but it's worth it. It's worth it because when we suffer for loving others, we never suffer alone. Instead, Peter tells us that when we suffer for love, we actually share with Christ in his sufferings. Because of what Jesus has done on the cross, suffering has ceased to be an enemy to be avoided and has become an ally that is able to bring us closer to our precious Savior. Lewis makes this point when he writes,

> Christ did not teach and suffer that we might become, even in the natural loves, more careful of our own happiness. . . . We shall draw nearer to God, not by trying to avoid the suffering inherent in all loves, but by accepting them and offering them to him; throwing away all defensive armor. If our hearts need to be broken, and if he chooses this as the way in which they should break, so be it.[20]

Let's be honest: Our hearts need to be broken. If we are ever to share with Christ in his sufferings, our hearts will

20. Ibid., 170.

need to be broken, and if God wants to use loving one another earnestly to break them, so be it. Better a broken heart with Jesus than an unbreakable heart without him. Only those who have shared with Christ in his sufferings will be able to rejoice and be glad when his glory is revealed.

You see, love won't always break our hearts. One day, every tear will be wiped away, all suffering will cease, and the sin that has plagued our relationships for so long will disappear. Then we will behold the glory of our Savior face to face, and together with all God's people we will be glad and rejoice forever.

Preparing for Tribulation

Now you may wonder what this chapter on loving one another is doing in a book focused on preparing you for the day of opposition. The reason I felt compelled to write this chapter is because I think that one of the best ways to prepare our hearts for external opposition is for Christians to love one another earnestly even when it's hard. Certainly, we will never be able to love our enemies when they persecute us if we can't love our brothers and sisters when they fail us.

However, if we will only love one another the way that our Savior has loved us, then we can join our brothers and sisters around the world in sharing in Christ's suffering. You don't have to move across the globe to take a risk, and you don't have to use your imagination to know how you will respond in the day of opposition.

Lay down your defensive armor, lean in where you have been pulling back, let go of what you have been holding onto, forgive the way you have been forgiven, love the way that you have been loved. If you will do that, then when the day of opposition comes, you will be ready to love your enemies and pray for those who persecute you.

And even before that day comes, by loving one another this way, you will have plenty of opportunities to share in the sufferings of our great Savior. "After you have suffered a little while, the God of all grace, who has called you to his eternal glory in Christ, will himself restore, confirm, strengthen, and establish you. To him be the dominion forever and ever. Amen" (1 Pet. 5:10–11).

*There followed him a great multitude of the people
and of women who were mourning and lamenting for him.
But turning to them Jesus said,
"Daughters of Jerusalem, do not weep for me,
but weep for yourselves and for your children."*
–Luke 23:27–28

9

DON'T WEEP FOR JESUS

Suffering, Joy, and the Glory to Come

Bob Blincoe

Beaten and belittled, the Lord Christ pulled himself outside the city towards his destiny, to give his life for the world. Down the *Via Dolorosa*, Jesus took step after deliberate step nearer to his death. The whole world was watching.

Some women were overcome by grief. They beat themselves and wept. Twice in my years of living in the Middle East, I saw weeping women beat themselves on account of some terrible personal loss. Our Lord stopped, and spoke to these weeping women. "Daughters of Jerusalem, don't weep for me."

What did Jesus mean? What was his hope? His hope was in his Father's love, in his Father's kingdom, and in the glory that his Father would reveal. It was God's love that enabled him to trust in his Father when the time of his own death drew near. He knew that the women did not need to weep for him because he would soon for the joy set before him, endure the cross, despising the shame, and sit down at the right hand of the throne of God (Heb. 12:2)

Our Resource for the Risk

Because churches are sending their sons and daughters as missionaries, we need to think deeply about Jesus Christ's understanding of God's love. If we are going to send our sons and daughters to the distant places and, in some cases, to the very gates of hell, we must have a theology of faith, hope, and love to sustain us when some of them die. We learn this theology from Jesus himself, who encouraged us to trust in our Father's love and not be surprised at a martyr's death.

Thinking deeply about God's love enables missionaries to do God's will in risky places. "Because your steadfast love is better than life, my lips will praise you" (Ps. 63:3). This is no side issue, but central to the teaching of the apostles. "Do not love the world or the things that are in the world. If anyone loves the world, the love of the Father is not in him" (1 John 2:15). Thomas Chalmers, Scotland's greatest nineteenth-century church leader, set forth his thoughts on this verse in his remarkable essay, "The Expulsive Power of a New Affection." Chalmers wrote, "The love of the world cannot be expunged by a mere demonstration of the world's worthlessness. But may it not be supplanted by the love of that which is more worthy of itself?" That is, a new affection, for something more highly prized, will drive out one's love for the things of the world.

Missionary families can think deeply about God's love, until God himself is the new affection that more than compensates for their losses. In him, they will lack nothing, and will gain everything. So, too, every husband and wife and every unmarried Christian must count on the guarantee of God's priceless love, and let this "new affection" expel less worthy aspirations. That is the way Jesus Christ lived by faith; that is the example he leaves for church leaders who have the responsibility of preparing their members to go and make disciples everywhere.

PLAY THE MAN

Roland and Becca were missionaries in Lebanon. Roland was a dedicated evangelist. He made it his practice to open his Arabic Bible and speak of Jesus Christ to Muslims every day. Then the region descended into chaos; months of lawlessness disturbed their city, when Muslim factions began blowing up cars.

During those days, when Roland would leave the house in the morning, Becca would walk with him to his car. She would say, "I love you." While she sat in the passenger seat, Roland would put the key in the ignition and turn on the car.

If nothing happened, that was the all clear.

Then, Becca would open the car door and return to their home, while Roland drove to his appointment. What courage it took for this couple to continue in the obedience of the Great Commission.

There are inspiring stories of Christian martyrs who gave a good account at their death. Hugh Latimer (who died October 16, 1555) was a British clergyman, Bishop of Worcester, and Protestant martyr during the reign of Mary I of England. Latimer was burnt at the stake.

As the executioner lit the wood, Latimer turned to his friend Ridley, who also was to be killed, and said, "Be of good comfort, Master Ridley, and play the man! We shall this day light such a candle, by God's grace, in England, as I trust shall never be put out."[21]

The times in which these martyrs lived forced them to think deeply about God's love and will in the way that Christ had to think and pray at Gethsemane and on the road to the cross. His faith, as the joy set before him (Heb. 12:2), desiring to glorify his Father, sustained Christ in those moments of greatest trial. "Now my soul is troubled, and what shall I say? 'Father, save me from this hour'? No, it was for this very reason I came to this hour. Father, glorify your name!" (John 12:27–28a, NIV).

So I say with him, as he said to the women of Jerusalem, "Don't weep for Jesus." His death was not a tragedy, not some Greek drama in which the fates conspire to destroy a hero.

> Then a voice came from heaven: "I have glorified it, and I will glorify it again." The crowd that stood there and heard it said that it had thundered. Others said, "An angel has spoken to him." Jesus answered, "This voice has come for your sake, not mine. Now is the judgment of this world; now will the ruler of this world be cast out. And I, when I am lifted up from the earth, will draw all people to myself." (John 12:28b–32)

Raised from the dead on the third day, Jesus ascended into heaven and sat down at the right hand of God the Father Almighty. From this exalted position in heaven, he began

21. John Fox, *Fox's Book of Martyrs: The Acts and Monuments of the Church*, vol. 3, edited by John Cumming (London: George Virtue, 1844), 492.

to call his beautiful bride from among all the peoples on our planet.

From that day until now, our Lord has been calling his bride to himself. And from that day, some missionaries have been called to be faithful and true unto death, to give to Jesus Christ their last full measure of devotion. These chosen few are called to suffer persecution and martyrdom.

Do we believe what the Bible has to say about the cost of discipleship? "It has been granted to you on behalf of Christ not only to believe in him, but also to suffer for him" (Phil. 1:29, NIV). Shall the church and her leaders send our sons and daughters only to the lands made fairly safe because yesterday's missionaries opened the work there?

For all the talk about completing the task of making disciples among "all the nations" (Greek *panta ta ethne),* most missionaries—and most missions dollars—go to improve Christianity where pioneer missionaries brought Christianity long ago. I have clicked through a thousand church websites in the last eight weeks. On the pull-down menus, churches usually feature their global missions program. A certain profile presents itself:

- Take a trip to the Holy Land
- Support missionaries in Uganda (85% Christian, English is the official language)
- Men's work trip to Mexico
- Give to national evangelists in India

I am not wishing to argue against any of these good things. But if you are holding back from sending your people to the hardest places out of fear, you will never obey Jesus's

Great Commission with God-glorifying obedience. Perfect fear casts out love.

The first priority—advancing into the demonic strongholds and rescuing the elect from the kingdom of darkness—has been replaced by making short-term visits to needy Christians or hiring evangelists we will never know to do the work of the gospel in places we would never go. Do we still take casualties? Or do we fear that we would have no good explanation of why "things went wrong" if our missionaries died?

Proven in the Fiery Trials

One of the most well known occasions of martyrdom in modern times, the death of Jim Elliot and Nate Saint and three other missionaries on a sandbar in the Curaray River in Ecuador, teaches us that the deaths of the martyrs is never in vain. (As I write, the sixtieth anniversary of their deaths on January 6, 1956, is approaching.) The missionaries went willingly, and never came back. Only recently have the Huaorani men of that tribe, now Christians, revealed what happened in the stillness that followed the murders. Nate's son, Steve Saint, wrote what they told him.

> Dawa, one of the three Huaorani women who watched while the missionaries were slain, told me that after the killing she saw *cowodi* above the trees, singing. She didn't know what this kind of music was until she later heard recordings of Aunt Rachel's and became familiar with the sound of a choir. Mincaya and Kimo confirmed that they heard the singing and saw

> what Dawa describes as angels along the ridge
> above the beach. Apparently all the participants
> saw this bright multitude in the sky and felt
> they should be scared, because they knew it was
> something supernatural.[22]

Dawa said that this supernatural experience was what drew her to God when she later heard of him.

In the stillness that followed death, the Huaorani people overheard the "welcome home" hymn of the heavenly choir. The Father's love was revealed to them through the devotion of those who were not surprised at suffering and rejoiced that they were counted worthy to suffer disgrace for his name.

On a recent trip to Kurdistan, Iraq, our taxi driver slowed down for an inspection at a government checkpoint. When we were cleared to drive down the road, the taxi driver said that we were within six miles of the ISIS army. "But there's a mountain between us and ISIS, so not to worry," he added. My admiration grew for Mark, my traveling companion, who was visiting Iraq for the first time. His daughter and her husband and their children live there in obedience to the Great Commission. Here is a father who daily has to press into the promises of God for the security of his daughter and her precious family. By the time we arrived at their home, we were only twenty miles from ISIS-held land.

22. Steve Saint, "Did They Have to Die?", *Christianity Today*, 16 September 1996.

This is a family with faith proven in the fiery trials. When Jesus's glory is revealed, they "will be glad also with exceeding joy" (1 Pet. 4:13, KJV).

Words from an Orange Jumpsuit

In Acts 7, we marvel at Stephen, a man glad with manifest joy, even as he became aware that he may have been speaking his final words. At the end of his words, Stephen saw heaven opened, and Jesus stood to receive him home.

Fast-forward to today, the image of a man in an orange jump suit kneeling and giving his final words. I have read that these men had been forced by their captors to rehearse their deaths many times. I do not know their thoughts at that moment, but I believe that, like Stephen, they knew their Lord stand for them, to welcome them into heaven.

But if it were me, the man in the orange jump suit, what would I want to say?

Perhaps my fears would overtake me and I would not have any courage at all, but if God gave me strength, here is what I would say.

> *Don't weep for me.*
> *The Lord is my light and my salvation—whom shall I fear?*
> *His loving kindness is better than life.*
> *Be it known to all that no murderer has eternal life in him.*
> *Father, forgive them, they don't know what they are doing.*

Behold, I see the Son of Man, standing at the right hand of God.
Who can separate us from the love of God? Shall tribulation or distress or persecution or nakedness or famine or peril or . . .

God's love is powerful enough to dispossess Christians of their fear of men. God's love is able to supplant our fear of sending sons and daughters to be frontline missionaries—and our fear of going ourselves.

When Jesus sent his disciples to preach the gospel everywhere, he promised them a reward great enough to compensate them for the hardships and death that they risked in obeying his Great Commission. To make up for their costly obedience, Jesus gave his cross-cultural missionaries a great advantage. He gave them the promise, "Behold, I am with you always, to the end of the age" (Matt. 28:20). There is no greater reward. The God-glorifying good that sustained Jesus at Gethsemane will keep our beloved missionaries when they are lonely, forsaken, expelled, sick, betrayed, arrested, or worse. Don't weep for them; they are partakers of Christ's sufferings. When his glory shall be revealed, they will be glad with exceeding joy.

In your hearts honor Christ the Lord as holy,
always being prepared to make a defense
to anyone who asks you for a reason
for the hope that is in you;
yet do it with gentleness and respect.
   −1 Peter 3:15

CONCLUSION

Will the World Ask about Your Hope?

John Piper

Why in 1 Peter 3:15 does the unbelieving world ask Christians about their hope? Peter tells us, "Always [be] prepared to make a defense to anyone who asks you for a *reason for the hope that is in you*" (1 Pet. 3:15). He doesn't say that they will ask about our faith. Or about our doctrine. Or even about our good conduct. They might ask those things. We want them to. But Peter is expecting that they will ask about our *hope*. Why?

Before we look at the answer in 1 Peter, let's define hope. *Hope is a heartfelt, joyful conviction that our short-term future is governed by an all-caring God, and our long-term future, beyond death, will be happy beyond imagination in the presence of the all-satisfying glory of God.* This definition will be evident in part one of our answer.

Why does the world ask about Christian hope? The answer has three parts.

1. VIBRANT, LIVING, UNSHAKABLE, BLOOD-BOUGHT HOPE
IS THE DEFINING MOTION OF THE BORN-AGAIN HEART,
THAT IS, THE CHRISTIAN HEART.

Peter begins his letter on this note: "According to [God's]
great mercy, he has caused us to be *born again to a living
hope* through the resurrection of Jesus Christ from the
dead" (1 Pet. 1:3). To be born again is to be alive with hope.

Hope is not an add-on to Christian experience. It is
part of the first things—the essential things. It is a vital
component of saving *faith*, because part of what we *believe*
relates to our future. It is impossible to be a Christian and
keep on believing that your eternity will be bleak. Saving
faith is the "assurance of things hoped for," and such faith
believes that God is the rewarder of "those who seek him"
(Heb. 11:1, 6).

Therefore, Peter is relentless in his letter to urge the
suffering exiles of the empire to fan the flame of their hope
to white-hot fullness.

The first command in his letter is "hope," modified
by the adverb "fully." "*Hope fully* on the grace that will be
brought to you at the revelation of Jesus Christ" (1 Pet.
1:13). The second coming of Jesus in glory is the earnest
hope of the believer's heart.

Peter had tasted the glory with Jesus on the Mount
of Transfiguration, and he knew it was a foretaste of the
second coming: "We made known to you the power and
coming of our Lord Jesus Christ . . . . [W]e were eyewit-
nesses of his majesty" (2 Pet. 1:16). He knew that he would
be "a partaker in the glory that is going to be revealed" (1
Pet. 5:1).

So he was passionate about wakening this hope fully in the beleaguered saints scattered through the empire. He promised the elders among them, "When the chief Shepherd appears, you will receive the unfading crown of glory" (1 Pet. 5:4). And he explained to the suffering saints that God's purpose in their sorrows is "that the tested genuineness of your faith . . . may be found to result in praise and glory and honor at the revelation of Jesus Christ" (1 Pet. 1:7). Their slander will be replaced with praise, their pain with glory, their shame with honor.

He tells them to hang on with hope for this short life, because soon all will be glorious: "After you have suffered a little while, the God of all grace, who has called you to his eternal glory in Christ, will himself restore, confirm, strengthen, and establish you" (1 Pet. 5:10).

This hope is absolutely sure because it was paid for by a ransom that is not perishable or cheap, but eternal and infinitely precious: "You were ransomed . . . not with perishable things such as silver or gold, but with the precious blood of Christ" (1 Pet. 1:18–19). So Peter urges the believers, with their blood-bought hope, to do the humanly impossible: "Rejoice insofar as you share Christ's sufferings, that you may also rejoice and be glad when his glory is revealed" (1 Pet. 4:13).

Short of that final day, there is this daily confidence in God's present care: "[Cast] all your anxieties on him, because he cares for you" (1 Pet. 5:7). He cares now. He will care tomorrow. And he will care forever. Therefore, part one of our answer to why the world asks about the Christian hope is that *vibrant, living, unshakable, blood-bought hope is the defining motion of the Christian heart.*

2. Authentic Christian hope gives rise to joyful
fearlessness in the face of human trouble and
threats.

This is the immediate context of 1 Peter 3:15 where Peter
says to be ready to give a reason for your hope. We'll start
in verse 14:

> Even if you should suffer for righteousness' sake,
> you will be blessed. *Have no fear of them, nor be
> troubled*, but in your hearts honor Christ the
> Lord as holy, always being prepared to make a
> defense to anyone who asks you for a reason for
> the hope that is in you.

It appears that the question about Christians' *hope* is
prompted by their perceived *fearlessness*. In Peter's mind
this makes perfect sense. Hope is the root of fearlessness.
You see this in the way Peter tells the wives to relate to
their unbelieving husbands. "The holy women who *hoped*
in God used to adorn themselves, by submitting to their
own husbands, as Sarah obeyed Abraham, calling him lord.
And you are her children, if you do good and *do not fear
anything that is frightening*" (1 Pet. 3:5–6). Godward hope
makes gutsy women. And men.

Hope is not directly visible. It is a *heartfelt* conviction.
Only God can see the heart directly. But when hope produces fearlessness, it is on the way to being visible. When
that fearlessness frees you to "rejoice insofar as you share
Christ's sufferings" (1 Pet. 4:13), your demeanor has now
become so counterintuitive, someone may want to ask you
a question.

Peter says that what they ask about is your hope. Which shows that, in his mind, the Christian life gives the impression to others that we are not hoping in what they are hoping in (security, comfort, approval, wealth). They do not know where our fearlessness and our joy in affliction are coming from. But they assume we have a hope different from theirs. They do not assume we are indifferent to a happy future. They just don't know what it is.

So the question from unbelievers about the Christian hope is explained, first, by the fact that *vibrant hope is the defining motion of the Christian heart*; and, second, because *authentic Christian hope gives rise to joyful fearlessness in the face of human trouble and threats.*

3. This fearless hope in the God of "great mercy" (1 Pet. 1:3) and "all grace" (1 Pet. 5:10) produces a life of overflowing good deeds that even the unbelieving world often finds irresistibly compelling.

If anything competes for prominence with the breath of hope in Peter's letter, it is the wind of good deeds. These good deeds do not simply refer to a Christian morality that avoids bad behaviors—though Peter regards that as essential: "[The time is past] for doing what the Gentiles want to do, living in sensuality, passions, drunkenness, orgies, drinking parties, and lawless idolatry. . . . Let none of you suffer as a murderer or a thief or an evildoer or as a meddler" (1 Pet. 4:3, 15).

Very few people are deeply impressed with a lifestyle that only avoids bad behaviors. This is essential. But Peter teaches that Christian hope gives rise to overflowing good

deeds that go way beyond avoiding bad deeds. The God
who gave us hope did so by "great mercy" and "all grace."
Therefore Peter's letter abounds with good deeds to unde-
serving people—even the very people who are hurting us.

"Do not repay evil for evil or reviling for reviling,
but on the contrary, bless, for to this you were called, that
you may obtain a blessing" (1 Pet. 3:9). Indeed, as we bless
those who revile us, it is possible, Peter says, to do it with
joy: "Rejoice insofar as you share Christ's sufferings" (1 Pet.
4:13).

This radically counterintuitive behavior is possible because of hope—specifically, hope in a Christ who "suffered
once for sins, the righteous for the unrighteous, that he
might bring us to God" (1 Pet. 3:18). He bought our hope,
and he modeled its fruit.

Returning good for evil is possible because of hope.
"If you are insulted for the name of Christ, you are blessed,
because the Spirit of glory and of God rests upon you" (1 Pet.
4:14). And that Spirit is there with you to comfort you, and
to assure you that the glory is coming.

It is not only joy that survives and thrives through the
mistreatment of others. So do good deeds. "If when you
do good and suffer for it you endure, this is a gracious thing
in the sight of God" (1 Pet. 2:20). "Let those who suffer
according to God's will entrust their souls to a faithful
Creator *while doing good*" (1 Pet. 4:19).

The triple goal in such good deeds is to silence ignorance, shame slanderers, and convert them all.

> This is the will of God, that by *doing good* you
> should <u>put to silence</u> the ignorance of foolish
> people. (1 Pet. 2:15)

> [Have] a good conscience, so that, when you are slandered, those who revile your *good behavior* in Christ may be <u>put to shame</u>. (1 Pet. 3:16)

> Keep your conduct among the Gentiles honorable, so that when they speak against you as evildoers, they may see your *good deeds* and <u>glorify God</u> on the day of visitation. (1 Pet. 2:12)

In other words, as God wills, there are good deeds that even the world must acknowledge are compelling. When those good deeds are done for the very ones who hurt us, they become more compelling. And when they are done with joy, they are almost irresistible. Someone is going to ask, "What are you hoping in?"

Therefore, Christians are not just casual about good deeds, but "*zealous* for what is good" (1 Pet. 3:13). That's why I said Christian hope produces a life of *overflowing* good deeds.

Pray They Would Ask

The burning question for the church today is: Does the world ask? If not, why not? Peter didn't say how often it would happen. He says be ready when it does. Surely God's Spirit creates seasons in history when the people of God are more hopeful, more fearless, and more merciful—and the world is more attentive and more disposed by God's grace to see reality.

Let us pray that such a season would be upon us. But you need not wait for the macro-shifts in the church and the world. There is hope to be enjoyed, fear to be defeated, and a good deed ready to be done—today.

ᛝ desiringGod

Everyone wants to be happy. Our website was born and built for happiness. We want people everywhere to understand and embrace the truth that God is most glorified in us when we are most satisfied in him. We've collected more than thirty years of John Piper's speaking and writing, including translations into more than forty languages. We also provide a daily stream of new written, audio, and video resources to help you find truth, purpose, and satisfaction that never end. And it's all available free of charge, thanks to the generosity of people who've been blessed by the ministry.

If you want more resources for true happiness, or if you want to learn more about our work at Desiring God, we invite you to visit us at www.desiringGod.org.

www.desiringGod.org

14721548R00071

Printed in Great Britain
by Amazon.co.uk, Ltd.,
Marston Gate.